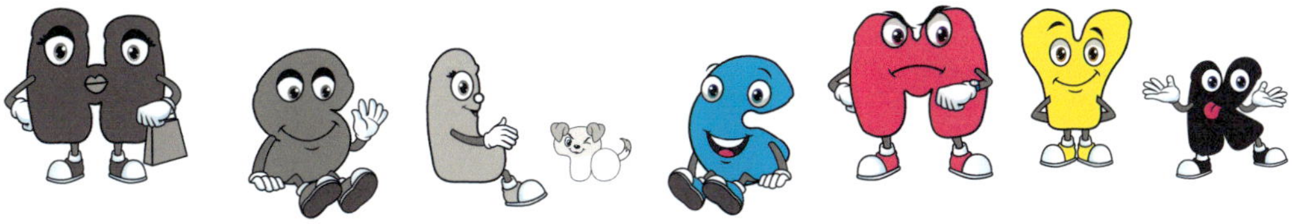

Color Charts for Indie Authors

Hard Copy Comparison Charts

Jenae Renee Jordan

Premium Color Ink
&
60# (100 GSM) White Paper

ISBN-13: 978-1949301175

Rhythm and Reasoning Publications, LLC

HSL

As an illustrator, there are times I prefer using the HSL color model versus either RGB or CMYK when creating my illustrations. For artwork featured in books that sell equally well in electronic and print formats, RGB is a good choice. However, CMYK generally is better for artwork featured in books that sell primarily in print format. For creations viewed mainly on electronic sources, HSL is without question my preferred choice.

The HSL color model works by manipulating hue, saturation, and lightness. Both RGB and CMYK work by combining colors. RGB using combinations of red, green, and blue. CMYK using cyan, magenta, yellow, and black.

Hue is pure color represented by degrees around a circle from 0 to 360. 0 corresponds with red, 40 with orange, 60 with yellow, 120 with green, 240 with blue, 300 with purple, and 360 with red.

The S value utilizes gray to adjust saturation. The value corresponding with pure color is 100. 0 corresponds with gray.

The L value adjusts the lightness of a color. The value corresponding with pure color is 50. 0 corresponds with black. 100 corresponds with white.

Developed in 1978, HSL was George Joblove's answer to creating a color model more in line with how humans perceive color versus how electronic sources create color. As humans, we tend to think of the three primary colors—red, blue, and yellow—as the basis for all other colors. For example, combining blue and yellow for green; yellow and red for orange; red and blue for purple—the secondary colors. Additionally, when it comes to the lightness or intensity of color, we tend to think in terms of gray scale manipulation versus color combinations.

HSL falls closer in line with our natural interpretation of color. But, just because HSL is easier to understand does not make it the correct choice for every project.

Besides artwork to be viewed mainly on electronic sources, when do I prefer HSL over RGB or CMYK? When creating realism, establishing moods, retro pieces, and illustrations for children with color sensitivity, to name a few.

Why? Ease of use for adjusting saturation and lightness—components utilized when creating these types of artwork. Why saturation and lightness are instrumental for these examples is an entirely different topic. The point is to show HSL may be better suited to particular compositions. RGB, CMYK, and HSL all have a place in my creative arsenal.

Most printers require CMYK press-ready files when processing digital artwork. So, why create using HSL if the files sent are CMYK press-ready? As mentioned above, ease of use during the creation process. Secondly, even though the files are processed using CMYK, color renders differently on the end product when using a color mode other than CMYK during the creation phase. Using HSL intentionally manipulates how colors appear on the printed end product.

H = 0, S = 0%, L = X%

(0, 0%, 100%)
(0%, 0%, 0%, 0%)

(0, 0%, 95%)
(0%, 0%, 0%, 5%)

(0, 0%, 90%)
(0%, 0%, 0%, 10%)

(0, 0%, 85%)
(0%, 0%, 0%, 15%)

(0, 0%, 80%)
(0%, 0%, 0%, 20%)

(0, 0%, 75%)
(0%, 0%, 0%, 25%)

(0, 0%, 70%)
(0%, 0%, 0%, 30%)

(0, 0%, 65%)
(0%, 0%, 0%, 35%)

(0, 0%, 60%)
(0%, 0%, 0%, 40%)

(0, 0%, 55%)
(0%, 0%, 0%, 45%)

(0, 0%, 50%)
(0%, 0%, 0%, 50%)

(0, 0%, 45%)
(0%, 0%, 0%, 55%)

(0, 0%, 40%)
(0%, 0%, 0%, 60%)

(0, 0%, 35%)
(0%, 0%, 0%, 65%)

(0, 0%, 30%)
(0%, 0%, 0%, 70%)

(0, 0%, 25%)
(0%, 0%, 0%, 75%)

(0, 0%, 20%)
(0%, 0%, 0%, 80%)

(0, 0%, 15%)
(0%, 0%, 0%, 85%)

(0, 0%, 10%)
(0%, 0%, 0%, 90%)

(0, 0%, 5%)
(0%, 0%, 0%, 95%)

(0, 0%, 0%)
(0%, 0%, 0%, 100%)

H = 0, S = X%, L = X%	H = 0, S = X%, L = 50%	H = 0, S = 100%, L = X%
(0, 100%, 100%) (0%, 0%, 0%, 0%)	(0, 100%, 50%) (0%, 100%, 100%, 0%)	(0, 100%, 100%) (0%, 0%, 0%, 0%)
(0, 95%, 95%) (0%, 10%, 10%, 0%)	(0, 95%, 50%) (0%, 97%, 97%, 3%)	(0, 100%, 95%) (0%, 10%, 10%, 0%)
(0, 90%, 90%) (0%, 18%, 18%, 1%)	(0, 90%, 50%) (0%, 95%, 95%, 5%)	(0, 100%, 90%) (0%, 20%, 20%, 0%)
(0, 85%, 85%) (0%, 26%, 26%, 2%)	(0, 85%, 50%) (0%, 92%, 92%, 7%)	(0, 100%, 85%) (0%, 30%, 30%, 0%)
(0, 80%, 80%) (0%, 33%, 33%, 4%)	(0, 80%, 50%) (0%, 89%, 89%, 10%)	(0, 100%, 80%) (0%, 40%, 40%, 0%)
(0, 75%, 75%) (0%, 40%, 40%, 6%)	(0, 75%, 50%) (0%, 86%, 86%, 13%)	(0, 100%, 75%) (0%, 50%, 50%, 0%)
(0, 70%, 70%) (0%, 46%, 46%, 9%)	(0, 70%, 50%) (0%, 82%, 82%, 15%)	(0, 100%, 70%) (0%, 60%, 60%, 0%)
(0, 65%, 65%) (0%, 52%, 52%, 12%)	(0, 65%, 50%) (0%, 79%, 79%, 18%)	(0, 100%, 65%) (0%, 70%, 70%, 0%)
(0, 60%, 60%) (0%, 57%, 57%, 16%)	(0, 60%, 50%) (0%, 75%, 75%, 20%)	(0, 100%, 60%) (0%, 80%, 80%, 0%)
(0, 55%, 55%) (0%, 62%, 62%, 20%)	(0, 55%, 50%) (0%, 71%, 71%, 22%)	(0, 100%, 55%) (0%, 90%, 90%, 0%)
(0, 50%, 50%) (0%, 67%, 67%, 25%)	(0, 50%, 50%) (0%, 67%, 67%, 25%)	(0, 100%, 50%) (0%, 100%, 100%, 0%)
(0, 45%, 45%) (0%, 62%, 62%, 35%)	(0, 45%, 50%) (0%, 62%, 62%, 28%)	(0, 100%, 45%) (0%, 100%, 100%, 10%)
(0, 40%, 40%) (0%, 57%, 57%, 44%)	(0, 40%, 50%) (0%, 57%, 57%, 30%)	(0, 100%, 40%) (0%, 100%, 100%, 20%)
(0, 35%, 35%) (0%, 52%, 52%, 53%)	(0, 35%, 50%) (0%, 52%, 52%, 32%)	(0, 100%, 35%) (0%, 100%, 100%, 30%)
(0, 30%, 30%) (0%, 46%, 46%, 61%)	(0, 30%, 50%) (0%, 46%, 46%, 35%)	(0, 100%, 30%) (0%, 100%, 100%, 40%)
(0, 25%, 25%) (0%, 40%, 40%, 69%)	(0, 25%, 50%) (0%, 40%, 40%, 38%)	(0, 100%, 25%) (0%, 100%, 100%, 50%)
(0, 20%, 20%) (0%, 33%, 33%, 76%)	(0, 20%, 50%) (0%, 33%, 33%, 40%)	(0, 100%, 20%) (0%, 100%, 100%, 60%)
(0, 15%, 15%) (0%, 26%, 26%, 83%)	(0, 15%, 50%) (0%, 26%, 26%, 43%)	(0, 100%, 15%) (0%, 100%, 100%, 70%)
(0, 10%, 10%) (0%, 18%, 18%, 89%)	(0, 10%, 50%) (0%, 18%, 18%, 45%)	(0, 100%, 10%) (0%, 100%, 100%, 80%)
(0, 5%, 5%) (0%, 10%, 10%, 95%)	(0, 5%, 50%) (0%, 10%, 10%, 47%)	(0, 100%, 5%) (0%, 100%, 100%, 90%)
(0, 0%, 0%) (0%, 0%, 0%, 100%)	(0, 0%, 50%) (0%, 0%, 0%, 50%)	(0, 100%, 0%) (0%, 0%, 0%, 100%)

H = 5, S = 100%, L = X%	H = 5, S = X%, L = 50%	H = 5, S = X%, L = X%
(5, 100%, 100%) (0%, 0%, 0%, 0%)	(5, 100%, 50%) (0%, 92%, 100%, 0%)	(5, 100%, 100%) (0%, 0%, 0%, 0%)
(5, 100%, 95%) (0%, 9%, 10%, 0%)	(5, 95%, 50%) (0%, 89%, 97%, 3%)	(5, 95%, 95%) (0%, 9%, 10%, 0%)
(5, 100%, 90%) (0%, 18%, 20%, 0%)	(5, 90%, 50%) (0%, 87%, 95%, 5%)	(5, 90%, 90%) (0%, 17%, 18%, 1%)
(5, 100%, 85%) (0%, 28%, 30%, 0%)	(5, 85%, 50%) (0%, 84%, 92%, 7%)	(5, 85%, 85%) (0%, 24%, 26%, 2%)
(5, 100%, 80%) (0%, 37%, 40%, 0%)	(5, 80%, 50%) (0%, 81%, 89%, 10%)	(5, 80%, 80%) (0%, 31%, 33%, 4%)
(5, 100%, 75%) (0%, 46%, 50%, 0%)	(5, 75%, 50%) (0%, 79%, 86%, 13%)	(5, 75%, 75%) (0%, 37%, 40%, 6%)
(5, 100%, 70%) (0%, 55%, 60%, 0%)	(5, 70%, 50%) (0%, 75%, 82%, 15%)	(5, 70%, 70%) (0%, 42%, 46%, 9%)
(5, 100%, 65%) (0%, 64%, 70%, 0%)	(5, 65%, 50%) (0%, 72%, 79%, 18%)	(5, 65%, 65%) (0%, 48%, 52%, 12%)
(5, 100%, 60%) (0%, 73%, 80%, 0%)	(5, 60%, 50%) (0%, 69%, 75%, 20%)	(5, 60%, 60%) (0%, 52%, 57%, 16%)
(5, 100%, 55%) (0%, 82%, 90%, 0%)	(5, 55%, 50%) (0%, 65%, 71%, 22%)	(5, 55%, 55%) (0%, 57%, 62%, 20%)
(5, 100%, 50%) (0%, 92%, 100%, 0%)	(5, 50%, 50%) (0%, 61%, 67%, 25%)	(5, 50%, 50%) (0%, 61%, 67%, 25%)
(5, 100%, 45%) (0%, 92%, 100%, 10%)	(5, 45%, 50%) (0%, 57%, 62%, 28%)	(5, 45%, 45%) (0%, 57%, 62%, 35%)
(5, 100%, 40%) (0%, 92%, 100%, 20%)	(5, 40%, 50%) (0%, 52%, 57%, 30%)	(5, 40%, 40%) (0%, 52%, 57%, 44%)
(5, 100%, 35%) (0%, 92%, 100%, 30%)	(5, 35%, 50%) (0%, 48%, 52%, 32%)	(5, 35%, 35%) (0%, 48%, 52%, 53%)
(5, 100%, 30%) (0%, 92%, 100%, 40%)	(5, 30%, 50%) (0%, 42%, 46%, 35%)	(5, 30%, 30%) (0%, 42%, 46%, 61%)
(5, 100%, 25%) (0%, 92%, 100%, 50%)	(5, 25%, 50%) (0%, 37%, 40%, 38%)	(5, 25%, 25%) (0%, 37%, 40%, 69%)
(5, 100%, 20%) (0%, 92%, 100%, 60%)	(5, 20%, 50%) (0%, 31%, 33%, 40%)	(5, 20%, 20%) (0%, 31%, 33%, 76%)
(5, 100%, 15%) (0%, 92%, 100%, 70%)	(5, 15%, 50%) (0%, 24%, 26%, 43%)	(5, 15%, 15%) (0%, 24%, 26%, 83%)
(5, 100%, 10%) (0%, 92%, 100%, 80%)	(5, 10%, 50%) (0%, 17%, 18%, 45%)	(5, 10%, 10%) (0%, 17%, 18%, 89%)
(5, 100%, 5%) (0%, 92%, 100%, 90%)	(5, 5%, 50%) (0%, 9%, 10%, 47%)	(5, 5%, 5%) (0%, 9%, 10%, 95%)
(5, 100%, 0%) (0%, 0%, 0%, 100%)	(5, 0%, 50%) (0%, 0%, 0%, 50%)	(5, 0%, 0%) (0%, 0%, 0%, 100%)

H = 10, S = X%, L = X%	H = 10, S = X%, L = 50%	H = 10, S = 100%, L = X%
(10, 100%, 100%) (0%, 0%, 0%, 0%)	(10, 100%, 50%) (0%, 83%, 100%, 0%)	(10, 100%, 100%) (0%, 0%, 0%, 0%)
(10, 95%, 95%) (0%, 8%, 10%, 0%)	(10, 95%, 50%) (0%, 81%, 97%, 3%)	(10, 100%, 95%) (0%, 8%, 10%, 0%)
(10, 90%, 90%) (0%, 15%, 18%, 1%)	(10, 90%, 50%) (0%, 79%, 95%, 5%)	(10, 100%, 90%) (0%, 17%, 20%, 0%)
(10, 85%, 85%) (0%, 22%, 26%, 2%)	(10, 85%, 50%) (0%, 77%, 92%, 7%)	(10, 100%, 85%) (0%, 25%, 30%, 0%)
(10, 80%, 80%) (0%, 28%, 33%, 4%)	(10, 80%, 50%) (0%, 74%, 89%, 10%)	(10, 100%, 80%) (0%, 33%, 40%, 0%)
(10, 75%, 75%) (0%, 33%, 40%, 6%)	(10, 75%, 50%) (0%, 71%, 86%, 13%)	(10, 100%, 75%) (0%, 42%, 50%, 0%)
(10, 70%, 70%) (0%, 38%, 46%, 9%)	(10, 70%, 50%) (0%, 69%, 82%, 15%)	(10, 100%, 70%) (0%, 50%, 60%, 0%)
(10, 65%, 65%) (0%, 43%, 52%, 12%)	(10, 65%, 50%) (0%, 66%, 79%, 18%)	(10, 100%, 65%) (0%, 58%, 70%, 0%)
(10, 60%, 60%) (0%, 48%, 57%, 16%)	(10, 60%, 50%) (0%, 63%, 75%, 20%)	(10, 100%, 60%) (0%, 67%, 80%, 0%)
(10, 55%, 55%) (0%, 52%, 62%, 20%)	(10, 55%, 50%) (0%, 59%, 71%, 22%)	(10, 100%, 55%) (0%, 75%, 90%, 0%)
(10, 50%, 50%) (0%, 56%, 67%, 25%)	(10, 50%, 50%) (0%, 56%, 67%, 25%)	(10, 100%, 50%) (0%, 83%, 100%, 0%)
(10, 45%, 45%) (0%, 52%, 62%, 35%)	(10, 45%, 50%) (0%, 52%, 62%, 28%)	(10, 100%, 45%) (0%, 83%, 100%, 10%)
(10, 40%, 40%) (0%, 48%, 57%, 44%)	(10, 40%, 50%) (0%, 48%, 57%, 30%)	(10, 100%, 40%) (0%, 83%, 100%, 20%)
(10, 35%, 35%) (0%, 43%, 52%, 53%)	(10, 35%, 50%) (0%, 43%, 52%, 32%)	(10, 100%, 35%) (0%, 83%, 100%, 30%)
(10, 30%, 30%) (0%, 38%, 46%, 61%)	(10, 30%, 50%) (0%, 38%, 46%, 35%)	(10, 100%, 30%) (0%, 83%, 100%, 40%)
(10, 25%, 25%) (0%, 33%, 40%, 69%)	(10, 25%, 50%) (0%, 33%, 40%, 38%)	(10, 100%, 25%) (0%, 83%, 100%, 50%)
(10, 20%, 20%) (0%, 28%, 33%, 76%)	(10, 20%, 50%) (0%, 28%, 33%, 40%)	(10, 100%, 20%) (0%, 83%, 100%, 60%)
(10, 15%, 15%) (0%, 22%, 26%, 83%)	(10, 15%, 50%) (0%, 22%, 26%, 43%)	(10, 100%, 15%) (0%, 83%, 100%, 70%)
(10, 10%, 10%) (0%, 15%, 18%, 89%)	(10, 10%, 50%) (0%, 15%, 18%, 45%)	(10, 100%, 10%) (0%, 83%, 100%, 80%)
(10, 5%, 5%) (0%, 8%, 10%, 95%)	(10, 5%, 50%) (0%, 8%, 10%, 47%)	(10, 100%, 5%) (0%, 83%, 100%, 90%)
(10, 0%, 0%) (0%, 0%, 0%, 100%)	(10, 0%, 50%) (0%, 0%, 0%, 50%)	(10, 100%, 0%) (0%, 0%, 0%, 100%)

H = 15, S = 100%, L = X%	H = 15, S = X%, L = 50%	H = 15, S = X%, L = X%
(15, 100%, 100%) (0%, 0%, 0%, 0%)	(15, 100%, 50%) (0%, 75%, 100%, 0%)	(15, 100%, 100%) (0%, 0%, 0%, 0%)
(15, 100%, 95%) (0%, 8%, 10%, 0%)	(15, 95%, 50%) (0%, 73%, 97%, 3%)	(15, 95%, 95%) (0%, 7%, 10%, 0%)
(15, 100%, 90%) (0%, 15%, 20%, 0%)	(15, 90%, 50%) (0%, 71%, 95%, 5%)	(15, 90%, 90%) (0%, 14%, 18%, 1%)
(15, 100%, 85%) (0%, 23%, 30%, 0%)	(15, 85%, 50%) (0%, 69%, 92%, 7%)	(15, 85%, 85%) (0%, 20%, 26%, 2%)
(15, 100%, 80%) (0%, 30%, 40%, 0%)	(15, 80%, 50%) (0%, 67%, 89%, 10%)	(15, 80%, 80%) (0%, 25%, 33%, 4%)
(15, 100%, 75%) (0%, 38%, 50%, 0%)	(15, 75%, 50%) (0%, 64%, 86%, 13%)	(15, 75%, 75%) (0%, 30%, 40%, 6%)
(15, 100%, 70%) (0%, 45%, 60%, 0%)	(15, 70%, 50%) (0%, 62%, 82%, 15%)	(15, 70%, 70%) (0%, 35%, 46%, 9%)
(15, 100%, 65%) (0%, 52%, 70%, 0%)	(15, 65%, 50%) (0%, 59%, 79%, 18%)	(15, 65%, 65%) (0%, 39%, 52%, 12%)
(15, 100%, 60%) (0%, 60%, 80%, 0%)	(15, 60%, 50%) (0%, 56%, 75%, 20%)	(15, 60%, 60%) (0%, 43%, 57%, 16%)
(15, 100%, 55%) (0%, 67%, 90%, 0%)	(15, 55%, 50%) (0%, 53%, 71%, 22%)	(15, 55%, 55%) (0%, 47%, 62%, 20%)
(15, 100%, 50%) (0%, 75%, 100%, 0%)	(15, 50%, 50%) (0%, 50%, 67%, 25%)	(15, 50%, 50%) (0%, 50%, 67%, 25%)
(15, 100%, 45%) (0%, 75%, 100%, 10%)	(15, 45%, 50%) (0%, 47%, 62%, 28%)	(15, 45%, 45%) (0%, 47%, 62%, 35%)
(15, 100%, 40%) (0%, 75%, 100%, 20%)	(15, 40%, 50%) (0%, 43%, 57%, 30%)	(15, 40%, 40%) (0%, 43%, 57%, 44%)
(15, 100%, 35%) (0%, 75%, 100%, 30%)	(15, 35%, 50%) (0%, 39%, 52%, 32%)	(15, 35%, 35%) (0%, 39%, 52%, 53%)
(15, 100%, 30%) (0%, 75%, 100%, 40%)	(15, 30%, 50%) (0%, 35%, 46%, 35%)	(15, 30%, 30%) (0%, 35%, 46%, 61%)
(15, 100%, 25%) (0%, 75%, 100%, 50%)	(15, 25%, 50%) (0%, 30%, 40%, 38%)	(15, 25%, 25%) (0%, 30%, 40%, 69%)
(15, 100%, 20%) (0%, 75%, 100%, 60%)	(15, 20%, 50%) (0%, 25%, 33%, 40%)	(15, 20%, 20%) (0%, 25%, 33%, 76%)
(15, 100%, 15%) (0%, 75%, 100%, 70%)	(15, 15%, 50%) (0%, 20%, 26%, 43%)	(15, 15%, 15%) (0%, 20%, 26%, 83%)
(15, 100%, 10%) (0%, 75%, 100%, 80%)	(15, 10%, 50%) (0%, 14%, 18%, 45%)	(15, 10%, 10%) (0%, 14%, 18%, 89%)
(15, 100%, 5%) (0%, 75%, 100%, 90%)	(15, 5%, 50%) (0%, 7%, 10%, 47%)	(15, 5%, 5%) (0%, 7%, 10%, 95%)
(15, 100%, 0%) (0%, 0%, 0%, 100%)	(15, 0%, 50%) (0%, 0%, 0%, 50%)	(15, 0%, 0%) (0%, 0%, 0%, 100%)

H = 20, S = X%, L = X%	H = 20, S = X%, L = 50%	H = 20, S = 100%, L = X%
(20, 100%, 100%) (0%, 0%, 0%, 0%)	(20, 100%, 50%) (0%, 67%, 100%, 0%)	(20, 100%, 100%) (0%, 0%, 0%, 0%)
(20, 95%, 95%) (0%, 6%, 10%, 0%)	(20, 95%, 50%) (0%, 65%, 97%, 3%)	(20, 100%, 95%) (0%, 7%, 10%, 0%)
(20, 90%, 90%) (0%, 12%, 18%, 1%)	(20, 90%, 50%) (0%, 63%, 95%, 5%)	(20, 100%, 90%) (0%, 13%, 20%, 0%)
(20, 85%, 85%) (0%, 17%, 26%, 2%)	(20, 85%, 50%) (0%, 61%, 92%, 7%)	(20, 100%, 85%) (0%, 20%, 30%, 0%)
(20, 80%, 80%) (0%, 22%, 33%, 4%)	(20, 80%, 50%) (0%, 59%, 89%, 10%)	(20, 100%, 80%) (0%, 27%, 40%, 0%)
(20, 75%, 75%) (0%, 27%, 40%, 6%)	(20, 75%, 50%) (0%, 57%, 86%, 13%)	(20, 100%, 75%) (0%, 33%, 50%, 0%)
(20, 70%, 70%) (0%, 31%, 46%, 9%)	(20, 70%, 50%) (0%, 55%, 82%, 15%)	(20, 100%, 70%) (0%, 40%, 60%, 0%)
(20, 65%, 65%) (0%, 35%, 52%, 12%)	(20, 65%, 50%) (0%, 53%, 79%, 18%)	(20, 100%, 65%) (0%, 47%, 70%, 0%)
(20, 60%, 60%) (0%, 38%, 57%, 16%)	(20, 60%, 50%) (0%, 50%, 75%, 20%)	(20, 100%, 60%) (0%, 53%, 80%, 0%)
(20, 55%, 55%) (0%, 41%, 62%, 20%)	(20, 55%, 50%) (0%, 47%, 71%, 22%)	(20, 100%, 55%) (0%, 60%, 90%, 0%)
(20, 50%, 50%) (0%, 44%, 67%, 25%)	(20, 50%, 50%) (0%, 44%, 67%, 25%)	(20, 100%, 50%) (0%, 67%, 100%, 0%)
(20, 45%, 45%) (0%, 41%, 62%, 35%)	(20, 45%, 50%) (0%, 41%, 62%, 28%)	(20, 100%, 45%) (0%, 67%, 100%, 10%)
(20, 40%, 40%) (0%, 38%, 57%, 44%)	(20, 40%, 50%) (0%, 38%, 57%, 30%)	(20, 100%, 40%) (0%, 67%, 100%, 20%)
(20, 35%, 35%) (0%, 35%, 52%, 53%)	(20, 35%, 50%) (0%, 35%, 52%, 32%)	(20, 100%, 35%) (0%, 67%, 100%, 30%)
(20, 30%, 30%) (0%, 31%, 46%, 61%)	(20, 30%, 50%) (0%, 31%, 46%, 35%)	(20, 100%, 30%) (0%, 67%, 100%, 40%)
(20, 25%, 25%) (0%, 27%, 40%, 69%)	(20, 25%, 50%) (0%, 27%, 40%, 38%)	(20, 100%, 25%) (0%, 67%, 100%, 50%)
(20, 20%, 20%) (0%, 22%, 33%, 76%)	(20, 20%, 50%) (0%, 22%, 33%, 40%)	(20, 100%, 20%) (0%, 67%, 100%, 60%)
(20, 15%, 15%) (0%, 17%, 26%, 83%)	(20, 15%, 50%) (0%, 17%, 26%, 43%)	(20, 100%, 15%) (0%, 67%, 100%, 70%)
(20, 10%, 10%) (0%, 12%, 18%, 89%)	(20, 10%, 50%) (0%, 12%, 18%, 45%)	(20, 100%, 10%) (0%, 67%, 100%, 80%)
(20, 5%, 5%) (0%, 6%, 10%, 95%)	(20, 5%, 50%) (0%, 6%, 10%, 47%)	(20, 100%, 5%) (0%, 67%, 100%, 90%)
(20, 0%, 0%) (0%, 0%, 0%, 100%)	(20, 0%, 50%) (0%, 0%, 0%, 50%)	(20, 100%, 0%) (0%, 0%, 0%, 100%)

H = 25, S = 100%, L = X%	H = 25, S = X%, L = 50%	H = 25, S = X%, L = X%
(25, 100%, 100%) (0%, 0%, 0%, 0%)	(25, 100%, 50%) (0%, 58%, 100%, 0%)	(25, 100%, 100%) (0%, 0%, 0%, 0%)
(25, 100%, 95%) (0%, 6%, 10%, 0%)	(25, 95%, 50%) (0%, 57%, 97%, 3%)	(25, 95%, 95%) (0%, 6%, 10%, 0%)
(25, 100%, 90%) (0%, 12%, 20%, 0%)	(25, 90%, 50%) (0%, 55%, 95%, 5%)	(25, 90%, 90%) (0%, 11%, 18%, 1%)
(25, 100%, 85%) (0%, 18%, 30%, 0%)	(25, 85%, 50%) (0%, 54%, 92%, 7%)	(25, 85%, 85%) (0%, 15%, 26%, 2%)
(25, 100%, 80%) (0%, 23%, 40%, 0%)	(25, 80%, 50%) (0%, 52%, 89%, 10%)	(25, 80%, 80%) (0%, 19%, 33%, 4%)
(25, 100%, 75%) (0%, 29%, 50%, 0%)	(25, 75%, 50%) (0%, 50%, 86%, 13%)	(25, 75%, 75%) (0%, 23%, 40%, 6%)
(25, 100%, 70%) (0%, 35%, 60%, 0%)	(25, 70%, 50%) (0%, 48%, 82%, 15%)	(25, 70%, 70%) (0%, 27%, 46%, 9%)
(25, 100%, 65%) (0%, 41%, 70%, 0%)	(25, 65%, 50%) (0%, 46%, 79%, 18%)	(25, 65%, 65%) (0%, 30%, 52%, 12%)
(25, 100%, 60%) (0%, 47%, 80%, 0%)	(25, 60%, 50%) (0%, 44%, 75%, 20%)	(25, 60%, 60%) (0%, 33%, 57%, 16%)
(25, 100%, 55%) (0%, 52%, 90%, 0%)	(25, 55%, 50%) (0%, 41%, 71%, 22%)	(25, 55%, 55%) (0%, 36%, 62%, 20%)
(25, 100%, 50%) (0%, 58%, 100%, 0%)	(25, 50%, 50%) (0%, 39%, 67%, 25%)	(25, 50%, 50%) (0%, 39%, 67%, 25%)
(25, 100%, 45%) (0%, 58%, 100%, 10%)	(25, 45%, 50%) (0%, 36%, 62%, 28%)	(25, 45%, 45%) (0%, 36%, 62%, 35%)
(25, 100%, 40%) (0%, 58%, 100%, 20%)	(25, 40%, 50%) (0%, 33%, 57%, 30%)	(25, 40%, 40%) (0%, 33%, 57%, 44%)
(25, 100%, 35%) (0%, 58%, 100%, 30%)	(25, 35%, 50%) (0%, 30%, 52%, 32%)	(25, 35%, 35%) (0%, 30%, 52%, 53%)
(25, 100%, 30%) (0%, 58%, 100%, 40%)	(25, 30%, 50%) (0%, 27%, 46%, 35%)	(25, 30%, 30%) (0%, 27%, 46%, 61%)
(25, 100%, 25%) (0%, 58%, 100%, 50%)	(25, 25%, 50%) (0%, 23%, 40%, 38%)	(25, 25%, 25%) (0%, 23%, 40%, 69%)
(25, 100%, 20%) (0%, 58%, 100%, 60%)	(25, 20%, 50%) (0%, 19%, 33%, 40%)	(25, 20%, 20%) (0%, 19%, 33%, 76%)
(25, 100%, 15%) (0%, 58%, 100%, 70%)	(25, 15%, 50%) (0%, 15%, 26%, 43%)	(25, 15%, 15%) (0%, 15%, 26%, 83%)
(25, 100%, 10%) (0%, 58%, 100%, 80%)	(25, 10%, 50%) (0%, 11%, 18%, 45%)	(25, 10%, 10%) (0%, 11%, 18%, 89%)
(25, 100%, 5%) (0%, 58%, 100%, 90%)	(25, 5%, 50%) (0%, 6%, 10%, 47%)	(25, 5%, 5%) (0%, 6%, 10%, 95%)
(25, 100%, 0%) (0%, 0%, 0%, 100%)	(25, 0%, 50%) (0%, 0%, 0%, 50%)	(25, 0%, 0%) (0%, 0%, 0%, 100%)

H = 30, S = X%, L = X%	H = 30, S = X%, L = 50%	H = 30, S = 100%, L = X%
(30, 100%, 100%) (0%, 0%, 0%, 0%)	(30, 100%, 50%) (0%, 50%, 100%, 0%)	(30, 100%, 100%) (0%, 0%, 0%, 0%)
(30, 95%, 95%) (0%, 5%, 10%, 0%)	(30, 95%, 50%) (0%, 49%, 97%, 3%)	(30, 100%, 95%) (0%, 5%, 10%, 0%)
(30, 90%, 90%) (0%, 9%, 18%, 1%)	(30, 90%, 50%) (0%, 47%, 95%, 5%)	(30, 100%, 90%) (0%, 10%, 20%, 0%)
(30, 85%, 85%) (0%, 13%, 26%, 2%)	(30, 85%, 50%) (0%, 46%, 92%, 7%)	(30, 100%, 85%) (0%, 15%, 30%, 0%)
(30, 80%, 80%) (0%, 17%, 33%, 4%)	(30, 80%, 50%) (0%, 44%, 89%, 10%)	(30, 100%, 80%) (0%, 20%, 40%, 0%)
(30, 75%, 75%) (0%, 20%, 40%, 6%)	(30, 75%, 50%) (0%, 43%, 86%, 13%)	(30, 100%, 75%) (0%, 25%, 50%, 0%)
(30, 70%, 70%) (0%, 23%, 46%, 9%)	(30, 70%, 50%) (0%, 41%, 82%, 15%)	(30, 100%, 70%) (0%, 30%, 60%, 0%)
(30, 65%, 65%) (0%, 26%, 52%, 12%)	(30, 65%, 50%) (0%, 36%, 79%, 18%)	(30, 100%, 65%) (0%, 35%, 70%, 0%)
(30, 60%, 60%) (0%, 29%, 57%, 16%)	(30, 60%, 50%) (0%, 38%, 75%, 20%)	(30, 100%, 60%) (0%, 40%, 80%, 0%)
(30, 55%, 55%) (0%, 31%, 62%, 20%)	(30, 55%, 50%) (0%, 35%, 71%, 22%)	(30, 100%, 55%) (0%, 45%, 90%, 0%)
(30, 50%, 50%) (0%, 33%, 67%, 25%)	(30, 50%, 50%) (0%, 33%, 67%, 25%)	(30, 100%, 50%) (0%, 50%, 100%, 0%)
(30, 45%, 45%) (0%, 31%, 62%, 35%)	(30, 45%, 50%) (0%, 31%, 62%, 28%)	(30, 100%, 45%) (0%, 50%, 100%, 10%)
(30, 40%, 40%) (0%, 29%, 57%, 44%)	(30, 40%, 50%) (0%, 29%, 57%, 30%)	(30, 100%, 40%) (0%, 50%, 100%, 20%)
(30, 35%, 35%) (0%, 26%, 52%, 53%)	(30, 35%, 50%) (0%, 26%, 52%, 32%)	(30, 100%, 35%) (0%, 50%, 100%, 30%)
(30, 30%, 30%) (0%, 23%, 46%, 61%)	(30, 30%, 50%) (0%, 23%, 46%, 35%)	(30, 100%, 30%) (0%, 50%, 100%, 40%)
(30, 25%, 25%) (0%, 20%, 40%, 69%)	(30, 25%, 50%) (0%, 20%, 40%, 38%)	(30, 100%, 25%) (0%, 50%, 100%, 50%)
(30, 20%, 20%) (0%, 17%, 33%, 76%)	(30, 20%, 50%) (0%, 17%, 33%, 40%)	(30, 100%, 20%) (0%, 50%, 100%, 60%)
(30, 15%, 15%) (0%, 13%, 26%, 83%)	(30, 15%, 50%) (0%, 13%, 26%, 43%)	(30, 100%, 15%) (0%, 50%, 100%, 70%)
(30, 10%, 10%) (0%, 9%, 18%, 89%)	(30, 10%, 50%) (0%, 9%, 18%, 45%)	(30, 100%, 10%) (0%, 50%, 100%, 80%)
(30, 5%, 5%) (0%, 5%, 10%, 95%)	(30, 5%, 50%) (0%, 5%, 10%, 47%)	(30, 100%, 5%) (0%, 50%, 100%, 90%)
(30, 0%, 0%) (0%, 0%, 0%, 100%)	(30, 0%, 50%) (0%, 0%, 0%, 50%)	(30, 100%, 0%) (0%, 0%, 0%, 100%)

H = 35, S = 100%, L = X%	H = 35, S = X%, L = 50%	H = 35, S = X%, L = X%
(35, 100%, 100%) (0%, 0%, 0%, 0%)	(35, 100%, 50%) (0%, 42%, 100%, 0%)	(35, 100%, 100%) (0%, 0%, 0%, 0%)
(35, 100%, 95%) (0%, 4%, 10%, 0%)	(35, 95%, 50%) (0%, 41%, 97%, 3%)	(35, 95%, 95%) (0%, 4%, 10%, 0%)
(35, 100%, 90%) (0%, 8%, 20%, 0%)	(35, 90%, 50%) (0%, 39%, 95%, 5%)	(35, 90%, 90%) (0%, 8%, 18%, 1%)
(35, 100%, 85%) (0%, 13%, 30%, 0%)	(35, 85%, 50%) (0%, 38%, 92%, 7%)	(35, 85%, 85%) (0%, 11%, 26%, 2%)
(35, 100%, 80%) (0%, 17%, 40%, 0%)	(35, 80%, 50%) (0%, 37%, 89%, 10%)	(35, 80%, 80%) (0%, 14%, 33%, 4%)
(35, 100%, 75%) (0%, 21%, 50%, 0%)	(35, 75%, 50%) (0%, 36%, 86%, 13%)	(35, 75%, 75%) (0%, 17%, 40%, 6%)
(35, 100%, 70%) (0%, 25%, 60%, 0%)	(35, 70%, 50%) (0%, 34%, 82%, 15%)	(35, 70%, 70%) (0%, 19%, 46%, 9%)
(35, 100%, 65%) (0%, 29%, 70%, 0%)	(35, 65%, 50%) (0%, 33%, 79%, 18%)	(35, 65%, 65%) (0%, 22%, 52%, 12%)
(35, 100%, 60%) (0%, 33%, 80%, 0%)	(35, 60%, 50%) (0%, 31%, 75%, 20%)	(35, 60%, 60%) (0%, 24%, 57%, 16%)
(35, 100%, 55%) (0%, 37%, 90%, 0%)	(35, 55%, 50%) (0%, 30%, 71%, 22%)	(35, 55%, 55%) (0%, 26%, 62%, 20%)
(35, 100%, 50%) (0%, 42%, 100%, 0%)	(35, 50%, 50%) (0%, 28%, 67%, 25%)	(35, 50%, 50%) (0%, 28%, 67%, 25%)
(35, 100%, 45%) (0%, 42%, 100%, 10%)	(35, 45%, 50%) (0%, 26%, 62%, 28%)	(35, 45%, 45%) (0%, 26%, 62%, 35%)
(35, 100%, 40%) (0%, 42%, 100%, 20%)	(35, 40%, 50%) (0%, 24%, 57%, 30%)	(35, 40%, 40%) (0%, 24%, 57%, 44%)
(35, 100%, 35%) (0%, 42%, 100%, 30%)	(35, 35%, 50%) (0%, 22%, 52%, 32%)	(35, 35%, 35%) (0%, 22%, 52%, 53%)
(35, 100%, 30%) (0%, 42%, 100%, 40%)	(35, 30%, 50%) (0%, 19%, 46%, 35%)	(35, 30%, 30%) (0%, 19%, 46%, 61%)
(35, 100%, 25%) (0%, 42%, 100%, 50%)	(35, 25%, 50%) (0%, 17%, 40%, 38%)	(35, 25%, 25%) (0%, 17%, 40%, 69%)
(35, 100%, 20%) (0%, 42%, 100%, 60%)	(35, 20%, 50%) (0%, 14%, 33%, 40%)	(35, 20%, 20%) (0%, 14%, 33%, 76%)
(35, 100%, 15%) (0%, 42%, 100%, 70%)	(35, 15%, 50%) (0%, 11%, 26%, 43%)	(35, 15%, 15%) (0%, 11%, 26%, 83%)
(35, 100%, 10%) (0%, 42%, 100%, 80%)	(35, 10%, 50%) (0%, 8%, 18%, 45%)	(35, 10%, 10%) (0%, 8%, 18%, 89%)
(35, 100%, 5%) (0%, 42%, 100%, 90%)	(35, 5%, 50%) (0%, 4%, 10%, 47%)	(35, 5%, 5%) (0%, 4%, 10%, 95%)
(35, 100%, 0%) (0%, 0%, 0%, 100%)	(35, 0%, 50%) (0%, 0%, 0%, 50%)	(35, 0%, 0%) (0%, 0%, 0%, 100%)

H = 40, S = X%, L = X%	H = 40, S = X%, L = 50%	H = 40, S = 100%, L = X%
(40, 100%, 100%) (0%, 0%, 0%, 0%)	(40, 100%, 50%) (0%, 33%, 100%, 0%)	(40, 100%, 100%) (0%, 0%, 0%, 0%)
(40, 95%, 95%) (0%, 3%, 10%, 0%)	(40, 95%, 50%) (0%, 32%, 97%, 3%)	(40, 100%, 95%) (0%, 3%, 10%, 0%)
(40, 90%, 90%) (0%, 6%, 18%, 1%)	(40, 90%, 50%) (0%, 32%, 95%, 5%)	(40, 100%, 90%) (0%, 7%, 20%, 0%)
(40, 85%, 85%) (0%, 9%, 26%, 2%)	(40, 85%, 50%) (0%, 31%, 92%, 7%)	(40, 100%, 85%) (0%, 10%, 30%, 0%)
(40, 80%, 80%) (0%, 11%, 33%, 4%)	(40, 80%, 50%) (0%, 30%, 89%, 10%)	(40, 100%, 80%) (0%, 13%, 40%, 0%)
(40, 75%, 75%) (0%, 13%, 40%, 6%)	(40, 75%, 50%) (0%, 29%, 86%, 13%)	(40, 100%, 75%) (0%, 17%, 50%, 0%)
(40, 70%, 70%) (0%, 15%, 46%, 9%)	(40, 70%, 50%) (0%, 27%, 82%, 15%)	(40, 100%, 70%) (0%, 20%, 60%, 0%)
(40, 65%, 65%) (0%, 17%, 52%, 12%)	(40, 65%, 50%) (0%, 26%, 79%, 18%)	(40, 100%, 65%) (0%, 23%, 70%, 0%)
(40, 60%, 60%) (0%, 19%, 57%, 16%)	(40, 60%, 50%) (0%, 25%, 75%, 20%)	(40, 100%, 60%) (0%, 27%, 80%, 0%)
(40, 55%, 55%) (0%, 21%, 62%, 20%)	(40, 55%, 50%) (0%, 24%, 71%, 22%)	(40, 100%, 55%) (0%, 30%, 90%, 0%)
(40, 50%, 50%) (0%, 22%, 67%, 25%)	(40, 50%, 50%) (0%, 22%, 67%, 25%)	(40, 100%, 50%) (0%, 33%, 100%, 0%)
(40, 45%, 45%) (0%, 21%, 62%, 35%)	(40, 45%, 50%) (0%, 21%, 62%, 28%)	(40, 100%, 45%) (0%, 33%, 100%, 10%)
(40, 40%, 40%) (0%, 19%, 57%, 44%)	(40, 40%, 50%) (0%, 19%, 57%, 30%)	(40, 100%, 40%) (0%, 33%, 100%, 20%)
(40, 35%, 35%) (0%, 17%, 52%, 53%)	(40, 35%, 50%) (0%, 17%, 52%, 32%)	(40, 100%, 35%) (0%, 33%, 100%, 30%)
(40, 30%, 30%) (0%, 15%, 46%, 61%)	(40, 30%, 50%) (0%, 15%, 46%, 35%)	(40, 100%, 30%) (0%, 33%, 100%, 40%)
(40, 25%, 25%) (0%, 13%, 40%, 69%)	(40, 25%, 50%) (0%, 13%, 40%, 38%)	(40, 100%, 25%) (0%, 33%, 100%, 50%)
(40, 20%, 20%) (0%, 11%, 33%, 76%)	(40, 20%, 50%) (0%, 11%, 33%, 40%)	(40, 100%, 20%) (0%, 33%, 100%, 60%)
(40, 15%, 15%) (0%, 9%, 26%, 83%)	(40, 15%, 50%) (0%, 9%, 26%, 43%)	(40, 100%, 15%) (0%, 33%, 100%, 70%)
(40, 10%, 10%) (0%, 6%, 18%, 89%)	(40, 10%, 50%) (0%, 6%, 18%, 45%)	(40, 100%, 10%) (0%, 33%, 100%, 80%)
(40, 5%, 5%) (0%, 3%, 10%, 95%)	(40, 5%, 50%) (0%, 3%, 10%, 47%)	(40, 100%, 5%) (0%, 33%, 100%, 90%)
(40, 0%, 0%) (0%, 0%, 0%, 100%)	(40, 0%, 50%) (0%, 0%, 0%, 50%)	(40, 100%, 0%) (0%, 0%, 0%, 100%)

H = 45, S = 100%, L = X%	H = 45, S = X%, L = 50%	H = 45, S = X%, L = X%
(45, 100%, 100%) (0%, 0%, 0%, 0%)	(45, 100%, 50%) (0%, 25%, 100%, 0%)	(45, 100%, 100%) (0%, 0%, 0%, 0%)
(45, 100%, 95%) (0%, 3%, 10%, 0%)	(45, 95%, 50%) (0%, 24%, 97%, 3%)	(45, 95%, 95%) (0%, 2%, 10%, 0%)
(45, 100%, 90%) (0%, 5%, 20%, 0%)	(45, 90%, 50%) (0%, 24%, 95%, 5%)	(45, 90%, 90%) (0%, 5%, 18%, 1%)
(45, 100%, 85%) (0%, 7%, 30%, 0%)	(45, 85%, 50%) (0%, 23%, 92%, 7%)	(45, 85%, 85%) (0%, 7%, 26%, 2%)
(45, 100%, 80%) (0%, 10%, 40%, 0%)	(45, 80%, 50%) (0%, 22%, 89%, 10%)	(45, 80%, 80%) (0%, 8%, 33%, 4%)
(45, 100%, 75%) (0%, 13%, 50%, 0%)	(45, 75%, 50%) (0%, 21%, 86%, 13%)	(45, 75%, 75%) (0%, 10%, 40%, 6%)
(45, 100%, 70%) (0%, 15%, 60%, 0%)	(45, 70%, 50%) (0%, 21%, 82%, 15%)	(45, 70%, 70%) (0%, 12%, 46%, 9%)
(45, 100%, 65%) (0%, 17%, 70%, 0%)	(45, 65%, 50%) (0%, 20%, 79%, 18%)	(45, 65%, 65%) (0%, 13%, 52%, 12%)
(45, 100%, 60%) (0%, 20%, 80%, 0%)	(45, 60%, 50%) (0%, 19%, 75%, 20%)	(45, 60%, 60%) (0%, 14%, 57%, 16%)
(45, 100%, 55%) (0%, 22%, 90%, 0%)	(45, 55%, 50%) (0%, 18%, 71%, 22%)	(45, 55%, 55%) (0%, 16%, 62%, 20%)
(45, 100%, 50%) (0%, 25%, 100%, 0%)	(45, 50%, 50%) (0%, 17%, 67%, 25%)	(45, 50%, 50%) (0%, 17%, 67%, 25%)
(45, 100%, 45%) (0%, 25%, 100%, 10%)	(45, 45%, 50%) (0%, 16%, 62%, 28%)	(45, 45%, 45%) (0%, 16%, 62%, 35%)
(45, 100%, 40%) (0%, 25%, 100%, 20%)	(45, 40%, 50%) (0%, 14%, 57%, 30%)	(45, 40%, 40%) (0%, 14%, 57%, 44%)
(45, 100%, 35%) (0%, 25%, 100%, 30%)	(45, 35%, 50%) (0%, 13%, 52%, 32%)	(45, 35%, 35%) (0%, 13%, 52%, 53%)
(45, 100%, 30%) (0%, 25%, 100%, 40%)	(45, 30%, 50%) (0%, 12%, 46%, 35%)	(45, 30%, 30%) (0%, 12%, 46%, 61%)
(45, 100%, 25%) (0%, 25%, 100%, 50%)	(45, 25%, 50%) (0%, 10%, 40%, 38%)	(45, 25%, 25%) (0%, 10%, 40%, 69%)
(45, 100%, 20%) (0%, 25%, 100%, 60%)	(45, 20%, 50%) (0%, 8%, 33%, 40%)	(45, 20%, 20%) (0%, 8%, 33%, 76%)
(45, 100%, 15%) (0%, 25%, 100%, 70%)	(45, 15%, 50%) (0%, 7%, 26%, 43%)	(45, 15%, 15%) (0%, 7%, 26%, 83%)
(45, 100%, 10%) (0%, 25%, 100%, 80%)	(45, 10%, 50%) (0%, 5%, 18%, 45%)	(45, 10%, 10%) (0%, 5%, 18%, 89%)
(45, 100%, 5%) (0%, 25%, 100%, 90%)	(45, 5%, 50%) (0%, 2%, 10%, 47%)	(45, 5%, 5%) (0%, 2%, 10%, 95%)
(45, 100%, 0%) (0%, 0%, 0%, 100%)	(45, 0%, 50%) (0%, 0%, 0%, 50%)	(45, 0%, 0%) (0%, 0%, 0%, 100%)

H = 50, S = X%, L = X%	H = 50, S = X%, L = 50%	H = 50, S = 100%, L = X%
(50, 100%, 100%) (0%, 0%, 0%, 0%)	(50, 100%, 50%) (0%, 17%, 100%, 0%)	(50, 100%, 100%) (0%, 0%, 0%, 0%)
(50, 95%, 95%) (0%, 2%, 10%, 0%)	(50, 95%, 50%) (0%, 16%, 97%, 3%)	(50, 100%, 95%) (0%, 2%, 10%, 0%)
(50, 90%, 90%) (0%, 3%, 18%, 1%)	(50, 90%, 50%) (0%, 16%, 95%, 5%)	(50, 100%, 90%) (0%, 3%, 20%, 0%)
(50, 85%, 85%) (0%, 4%, 26%, 2%)	(50, 85%, 50%) (0%, 15%, 92%, 7%)	(50, 100%, 85%) (0%, 5%, 30%, 0%)
(50, 80%, 80%) (0%, 6%, 33%, 4%)	(50, 80%, 50%) (0%, 15%, 89%, 10%)	(50, 100%, 80%) (0%, 7%, 40%, 0%)
(50, 75%, 75%) (0%, 7%, 40%, 6%)	(50, 75%, 50%) (0%, 14%, 86%, 13%)	(50, 100%, 75%) (0%, 8%, 50%, 0%)
(50, 70%, 70%) (0%, 8%, 46%, 9%)	(50, 70%, 50%) (0%, 14%, 82%, 15%)	(50, 100%, 70%) (0%, 10%, 60%, 0%)
(50, 65%, 65%) (0%, 9%, 52%, 12%)	(50, 65%, 50%) (0%, 13%, 79%, 18%)	(50, 100%, 65%) (0%, 12%, 70%, 0%)
(50, 60%, 60%) (0%, 10%, 57%, 16%)	(50, 60%, 50%) (0%, 12%, 75%, 20%)	(50, 100%, 60%) (0%, 13%, 80%, 0%)
(50, 55%, 55%) (0%, 10%, 62%, 20%)	(50, 55%, 50%) (0%, 12%, 71%, 22%)	(50, 100%, 55%) (0%, 15%, 90%, 0%)
(50, 50%, 50%) (0%, 11%, 67%, 25%)	(50, 50%, 50%) (0%, 11%, 67%, 25%)	(50, 100%, 50%) (0%, 17%, 100%, 0%)
(50, 45%, 45%) (0%, 10%, 62%, 35%)	(50, 45%, 50%) (0%, 10%, 62%, 28%)	(50, 100%, 45%) (0%, 17%, 100%, 10%)
(50, 40%, 40%) (0%, 10%, 57%, 44%)	(50, 40%, 50%) (0%, 10%, 57%, 30%)	(50, 100%, 40%) (0%, 17%, 100%, 20%)
(50, 35%, 35%) (0%, 9%, 52%, 53%)	(50, 35%, 50%) (0%, 9%, 52%, 32%)	(50, 100%, 35%) (0%, 17%, 100%, 30%)
(50, 30%, 30%) (0%, 8%, 46%, 61%)	(50, 30%, 50%) (0%, 8%, 46%, 35%)	(50, 100%, 30%) (0%, 17%, 100%, 40%)
(50, 25%, 25%) (0%, 7%, 40%, 69%)	(50, 25%, 50%) (0%, 7%, 40%, 38%)	(50, 100%, 25%) (0%, 17%, 100%, 50%)
(50, 20%, 20%) (0%, 6%, 33%, 76%)	(50, 20%, 50%) (0%, 6%, 33%, 40%)	(50, 100%, 20%) (0%, 17%, 100%, 60%)
(50, 15%, 15%) (0%, 4%, 26%, 83%)	(50, 15%, 50%) (0%, 4%, 26%, 43%)	(50, 100%, 15%) (0%, 17%, 100%, 70%)
(50, 10%, 10%) (0%, 3%, 18%, 89%)	(50, 10%, 50%) (0%, 3%, 18%, 45%)	(50, 100%, 10%) (0%, 17%, 100%, 80%)
(50, 5%, 5%) (0%, 2%, 10%, 95%)	(50, 5%, 50%) (0%, 2%, 10%, 47%)	(50, 100%, 5%) (0%, 17%, 100%, 90%)
(50, 0%, 0%) (0%, 0%, 0%, 100%)	(50, 0%, 50%) (0%, 0%, 0%, 50%)	(50, 100%, 0%) (0%, 0%, 0%, 100%)

H = 55, S = 100%, L = X%	H = 55, S = X%, L = 50%	H = 55, S = X%, L = X%
(55, 100%, 100%) (0%, 0%, 0%, 0%)	(55, 100%, 50%) (0%, 8%, 100%, 0%)	(55, 100%, 100%) (0%, 0%, 0%, 0%)
(55, 100%, 95%) (0%, 1%, 10%, 0%)	(55, 95%, 50%) (0%, 8%, 97%, 3%)	(55, 95%, 95%) (0%, 1%, 10%, 0%)
(55, 100%, 90%) (0%, 2%, 20%, 0%)	(55, 90%, 50%) (0%, 8%, 95%, 5%)	(55, 90%, 90%) (0%, 2%, 18%, 1%)
(55, 100%, 85%) (0%, 3%, 30%, 0%)	(55, 85%, 50%) (0%, 8%, 92%, 7%)	(55, 85%, 85%) (0%, 2%, 26%, 2%)
(55, 100%, 80%) (0%, 3%, 40%, 0%)	(55, 80%, 50%) (0%, 7%, 89%, 10%)	(55, 80%, 80%) (0%, 3%, 33%, 4%)
(55, 100%, 75%) (0%, 4%, 50%, 0%)	(55, 75%, 50%) (0%, 7%, 86%, 13%)	(55, 75%, 75%) (0%, 3%, 40%, 6%)
(55, 100%, 70%) (0%, 5%, 60%, 0%)	(55, 70%, 50%) (0%, 7%, 82%, 15%)	(55, 70%, 70%) (0%, 4%, 46%, 9%)
(55, 100%, 65%) (0%, 6%, 70%, 0%)	(55, 65%, 50%) (0%, 7%, 79%, 18%)	(55, 65%, 65%) (0%, 4%, 52%, 12%)
(55, 100%, 60%) (0%, 7%, 80%, 0%)	(55, 60%, 50%) (0%, 6%, 75%, 20%)	(55, 60%, 60%) (0%, 5%, 57%, 16%)
(55, 100%, 55%) (0%, 8%, 90%, 0%)	(55, 55%, 50%) (0%, 6%, 71%, 22%)	(55, 55%, 55%) (0%, 5%, 62%, 20%)
(55, 100%, 50%) (0%, 8%, 100%, 0%)	(55, 50%, 50%) (0%, 6%, 67%, 25%)	(55, 50%, 50%) (0%, 6%, 67%, 25%)
(55, 100%, 45%) (0%, 8%, 100%, 10%)	(55, 45%, 50%) (0%, 5%, 62%, 28%)	(55, 45%, 45%) (0%, 5%, 62%, 35%)
(55, 100%, 40%) (0%, 8%, 100%, 20%)	(55, 40%, 50%) (0%, 5%, 57%, 30%)	(55, 40%, 40%) (0%, 5%, 57%, 44%)
(55, 100%, 35%) (0%, 8%, 100%, 30%)	(55, 35%, 50%) (0%, 4%, 52%, 32%)	(55, 35%, 35%) (0%, 4%, 52%, 53%)
(55, 100%, 30%) (0%, 8%, 100%, 40%)	(55, 30%, 50%) (0%, 4%, 46%, 35%)	(55, 30%, 30%) (0%, 4%, 46%, 61%)
(55, 100%, 25%) (0%, 8%, 100%, 50%)	(55, 25%, 50%) (0%, 3%, 40%, 38%)	(55, 25%, 25%) (0%, 3%, 40%, 69%)
(55, 100%, 20%) (0%, 8%, 100%, 60%)	(55, 20%, 50%) (0%, 3%, 33%, 40%)	(55, 20%, 20%) (0%, 3%, 33%, 76%)
(55, 100%, 15%) (0%, 8%, 100%, 70%)	(55, 15%, 50%) (0%, 2%, 26%, 43%)	(55, 15%, 15%) (0%, 2%, 26%, 83%)
(55, 100%, 10%) (0%, 8%, 100%, 80%)	(55, 10%, 50%) (0%, 2%, 18%, 45%)	(55, 10%, 10%) (0%, 2%, 18%, 89%)
(55, 100%, 5%) (0%, 8%, 100%, 90%)	(55, 5%, 50%) (0%, 1%, 10%, 47%)	(55, 5%, 5%) (0%, 1%, 10%, 95%)
(55, 100%, 0%) (0%, 0%, 0%, 100%)	(55, 0%, 50%) (0%, 0%, 0%, 50%)	(55, 0%, 0%) (0%, 0%, 0%, 100%)

H = 60, S = X%, L = X%	H = 60, S = X%, L = 50%	H = 60, S = 100%, L = X%
(60, 100%, 100%) (0%, 0%, 0%, 0%)	(60, 100%, 50%) (0%, 0%, 100%, 0%)	(60, 100%, 100%) (0%, 0%, 0%, 0%)
(60, 95%, 95%) (0%, 0%, 10%, 0%)	(60, 95%, 50%) (0%, 0%, 97%, 3%)	(60, 100%, 95%) (0%, 0%, 10%, 0%)
(60, 90%, 90%) (0%, 0%, 18%, 1%)	(60, 90%, 50%) (0%, 0%, 95%, 5%)	(60, 100%, 90%) (0%, 0%, 20%, 0%)
(60, 85%, 85%) (0%, 0%, 26%, 2%)	(60, 85%, 50%) (0%, 0%, 92%, 7%)	(60, 100%, 85%) (0%, 0%, 30%, 0%)
(60, 80%, 80%) (0%, 0%, 33%, 4%)	(60, 80%, 50%) (0%, 0%, 89%, 10%)	(60, 100%, 80%) (0%, 0%, 40%, 0%)
(60, 75%, 75%) (0%, 0%, 40%, 6%)	(60, 75%, 50%) (0%, 0%, 86%, 13%)	(60, 100%, 75%) (0%, 0%, 50%, 0%)
(60, 70%, 70%) (0%, 0%, 46%, 9%)	(60, 70%, 50%) (0%, 0%, 82%, 15%)	(60, 100%, 70%) (0%, 0%, 60%, 0%)
(60, 65%, 65%) (0%, 0%, 52%, 12%)	(60, 65%, 50%) (0%, 0%, 79%, 18%)	(60, 100%, 65%) (0%, 0%, 70%, 0%)
(60, 60%, 60%) (0%, 0%, 57%, 16%)	(60, 60%, 50%) (0%, 0%, 75%, 20%)	(60, 100%, 60%) (0%, 0%, 80%, 0%)
(60, 55%, 55%) (0%, 0%, 62%, 20%)	(60, 55%, 50%) (0%, 0%, 71%, 22%)	(60, 100%, 55%) (0%, 0%, 90%, 0%)
(60, 50%, 50%) (0%, 0%, 67%, 25%)	(60, 50%, 50%) (0%, 0%, 67%, 25%)	(60, 100%, 50%) (0%, 0%, 100%, 0%)
(60, 45%, 45%) (0%, 0%, 62%, 35%)	(60, 45%, 50%) (0%, 0%, 62%, 28%)	(60, 100%, 45%) (0%, 0%, 100%, 10%)
(60, 40%, 40%) (0%, 0%, 57%, 44%)	(60, 40%, 50%) (0%, 0%, 57%, 30%)	(60, 100%, 40%) (0%, 0%, 100%, 20%)
(60, 35%, 35%) (0%, 0%, 52%, 53%)	(60, 35%, 50%) (0%, 0%, 52%, 32%)	(60, 100%, 35%) (0%, 0%, 100%, 30%)
(60, 30%, 30%) (0%, 0%, 46%, 61%)	(60, 30%, 50%) (0%, 0%, 46%, 35%)	(60, 100%, 30%) (0%, 0%, 100%, 40%)
(60, 25%, 25%) (0%, 0%, 40%, 69%)	(60, 25%, 50%) (0%, 0%, 40%, 38%)	(60, 100%, 25%) (0%, 0%, 100%, 50%)
(60, 20%, 20%) (0%, 0%, 33%, 76%)	(60, 20%, 50%) (0%, 0%, 33%, 40%)	(60, 100%, 20%) (0%, 0%, 100%, 60%)
(60, 15%, 15%) (0%, 0%, 26%, 83%)	(60, 15%, 50%) (0%, 0%, 26%, 43%)	(60, 100%, 15%) (0%, 0%, 100%, 70%)
(60, 10%, 10%) (0%, 0%, 18%, 89%)	(60, 10%, 50%) (0%, 0%, 18%, 45%)	(60, 100%, 10%) (0%, 0%, 100%, 80%)
(60, 5%, 5%) (0%, 0%, 10%, 95%)	(60, 5%, 50%) (0%, 0%, 10%, 47%)	(60, 100%, 5%) (0%, 0%, 100%, 90%)
(60, 0%, 0%) (0%, 0%, 0%, 100%)	(60, 0%, 50%) (0%, 0%, 0%, 50%)	(60, 100%, 0%) (0%, 0%, 0%, 100%)

H = 65, S = 100%, L = X%	H = 65, S = X%, L = 50%	H = 65, S = X%, L = X%
(65, 100%, 100%) (0%, 0%, 0%, 0%)	(65, 100%, 50%) (8%, 0%, 100%, 0%)	(65, 100%, 100%) (0%, 0%, 0%, 0%)
(65, 100%, 95%) (1%, 0%, 10%, 0%)	(65, 95%, 50%) (8%, 0%, 97%, 3%)	(65, 95%, 95%) (1%, 0%, 10%, 0%)
(65, 100%, 90%) (2%, 0%, 20%, 0%)	(65, 90%, 50%) (8%, 0%, 95%, 5%)	(65, 90%, 90%) (2%, 0%, 18%, 1%)
(65, 100%, 85%) (2%, 0%, 30%, 0%)	(65, 85%, 50%) (8%, 0%, 92%, 7%)	(65, 85%, 85%) (2%, 0%, 26%, 2%)
(65, 100%, 80%) (3%, 0%, 40%, 0%)	(65, 80%, 50%) (7%, 0%, 89%, 10%)	(65, 80%, 80%) (3%, 0%, 33%, 4%)
(65, 100%, 75%) (4%, 0%, 50%, 0%)	(65, 75%, 50%) (7%, 0%, 86%, 13%)	(65, 75%, 75%) (3%, 0%, 40%, 6%)
(65, 100%, 70%) (5%, 0%, 60%, 0%)	(65, 70%, 50%) (7%, 0%, 82%, 15%)	(65, 70%, 70%) (4%, 0%, 46%, 9%)
(65, 100%, 65%) (6%, 0%, 70%, 0%)	(65, 65%, 50%) (7%, 0%, 79%, 18%)	(65, 65%, 65%) (4%, 0%, 52%, 12%)
(65, 100%, 60%) (7%, 0%, 80%, 0%)	(65, 60%, 50%) (6%, 0%, 75%, 20%)	(65, 60%, 60%) (5%, 0%, 57%, 16%)
(65, 100%, 55%) (7%, 0%, 90%, 0%)	(65, 55%, 50%) (6%, 0%, 71%, 22%)	(65, 55%, 55%) (5%, 0%, 62%, 20%)
(65, 100%, 50%) (8%, 0%, 100%, 0%)	(65, 50%, 50%) (6%, 0%, 67%, 25%)	(65, 50%, 50%) (6%, 0%, 67%, 25%)
(65, 100%, 45%) (8%, 0%, 100%, 10%)	(65, 45%, 50%) (5%, 0%, 62%, 28%)	(65, 45%, 45%) (5%, 0%, 62%, 35%)
(65, 100%, 40%) (8%, 0%, 100%, 20%)	(65, 40%, 50%) (5%, 0%, 57%, 30%)	(65, 40%, 40%) (5%, 0%, 57%, 44%)
(65, 100%, 35%) (8%, 0%, 100%, 30%)	(65, 35%, 50%) (4%, 0%, 52%, 32%)	(65, 35%, 35%) (4%, 0%, 52%, 53%)
(65, 100%, 30%) (8%, 0%, 100%, 40%)	(65, 30%, 50%) (4%, 0%, 46%, 35%)	(65, 30%, 30%) (4%, 0%, 46%, 61%)
(65, 100%, 25%) (8%, 0%, 100%, 50%)	(65, 25%, 50%) (3%, 0%, 40%, 38%)	(65, 25%, 25%) (3%, 0%, 40%, 69%)
(65, 100%, 20%) (8%, 0%, 100%, 60%)	(65, 20%, 50%) (3%, 0%, 33%, 40%)	(65, 20%, 20%) (3%, 0%, 33%, 76%)
(65, 100%, 15%) (8%, 0%, 100%, 70%)	(65, 15%, 50%) (2%, 0%, 26%, 43%)	(65, 15%, 15%) (2%, 0%, 26%, 83%)
(65, 100%, 10%) (8%, 0%, 100%, 80%)	(65, 10%, 50%) (2%, 0%, 18%, 45%)	(65, 10%, 10%) (2%, 0%, 18%, 89%)
(65, 100%, 5%) (8%, 0%, 100%, 90%)	(65, 5%, 50%) (1%, 0%, 10%, 47%)	(65, 5%, 5%) (1%, 0%, 10%, 95%)
(65, 100%, 0%) (0%, 0%, 0%, 100%)	(65, 0%, 50%) (0%, 0%, 0%, 50%)	(65, 0%, 0%) (0%, 0%, 0%, 100%)

H = 70, S = X%, L = X%	H = 70, S = X%, L = 50%	H = 70, S = 100%, L = X%
(70, 100%, 100%) (0%, 0%, 0%, 0%)	(70, 100%, 50%) (17%, 0%, 100%, 0%)	(70, 100%, 100%) (0%, 0%, 0%, 0%)
(70, 95%, 95%) (2%, 0%, 10%, 0%)	(70, 95%, 50%) (16%, 0%, 97%, 3%)	(70, 100%, 95%) (2%, 0%, 10%, 0%)
(70, 90%, 90%) (3%, 0%, 18%, 1%)	(70, 90%, 50%) (16%, 0%, 95%, 5%)	(70, 100%, 90%) (3%, 0%, 20%, 0%)
(70, 85%, 85%) (4%, 0%, 26%, 2%)	(70, 85%, 50%) (15%, 0%, 92%, 7%)	(70, 100%, 85%) (5%, 0%, 30%, 0%)
(70, 80%, 80%) (6%, 0%, 33%, 4%)	(70, 80%, 50%) (15%, 0%, 89%, 10%)	(70, 100%, 80%) (7%, 0%, 40%, 0%)
(70, 75%, 75%) (7%, 0%, 40%, 6%)	(70, 75%, 50%) (14%, 0%, 86%, 13%)	(70, 100%, 75%) (8%, 0%, 50%, 0%)
(70, 70%, 70%) (8%, 0%, 46%, 9%)	(70, 70%, 50%) (14%, 0%, 82%, 15%)	(70, 100%, 70%) (10%, 0%, 60%, 0%)
(70, 65%, 65%) (9%, 0%, 52%, 12%)	(70, 65%, 50%) (13%, 0%, 79%, 18%)	(70, 100%, 65%) (12%, 0%, 70%, 0%)
(70, 60%, 60%) (10%, 0%, 57%, 16%)	(70, 60%, 50%) (13%, 0%, 75%, 20%)	(70, 100%, 60%) (13%, 0%, 80%, 0%)
(70, 55%, 55%) (10%, 0%, 62%, 20%)	(70, 55%, 50%) (12%, 0%, 71%, 22%)	(70, 100%, 55%) (15%, 0%, 90%, 0%)
(70, 50%, 50%) (11%, 0%, 67%, 25%)	(70, 50%, 50%) (11%, 0%, 67%, 25%)	(70, 100%, 50%) (17%, 0%, 100%, 0%)
(70, 45%, 45%) (10%, 0%, 62%, 35%)	(70, 45%, 50%) (10%, 0%, 62%, 28%)	(70, 100%, 45%) (17%, 0%, 100%, 10%)
(70, 40%, 40%) (10%, 0%, 57%, 44%)	(70, 40%, 50%) (10%, 0%, 57%, 30%)	(70, 100%, 40%) (17%, 0%, 100%, 20%)
(70, 35%, 35%) (9%, 0%, 52%, 53%)	(70, 35%, 50%) (9%, 0%, 52%, 32%)	(70, 100%, 35%) (17%, 0%, 100%, 30%)
(70, 30%, 30%) (8%, 0%, 46%, 61%)	(70, 30%, 50%) (8%, 0%, 46%, 35%)	(70, 100%, 30%) (17%, 0%, 100%, 40%)
(70, 25%, 25%) (7%, 0%, 40%, 69%)	(70, 25%, 50%) (7%, 0%, 40%, 38%)	(70, 100%, 25%) (17%, 0%, 100%, 50%)
(70, 20%, 20%) (6%, 0%, 33%, 76%)	(70, 20%, 50%) (6%, 0%, 33%, 40%)	(70, 100%, 20%) (17%, 0%, 100%, 60%)
(70, 15%, 15%) (4%, 0%, 26%, 83%)	(70, 15%, 50%) (4%, 0%, 26%, 43%)	(70, 100%, 15%) (17%, 0%, 100%, 70%)
(70, 10%, 10%) (3%, 0%, 18%, 89%)	(70, 10%, 50%) (3%, 0%, 18%, 45%)	(70, 100%, 10%) (17%, 0%, 100%, 80%)
(70, 5%, 5%) (2%, 0%, 10%, 95%)	(70, 5%, 50%) (2%, 0%, 10%, 47%)	(70, 100%, 5%) (17%, 0%, 100%, 90%)
(70, 0%, 0%) (0%, 0%, 0%, 100%)	(70, 0%, 50%) (0%, 0%, 0%, 50%)	(70, 100%, 0%) (0%, 0%, 0%, 100%)

H = 75, S = 100%, L = X%	H = 75, S = X%, L = 50%	H = 75, S = X%, L = X%
(75, 100%, 100%) (0%, 0%, 0%, 0%)	(75, 100%, 50%) (25%, 0%, 100%, 0%)	(75, 100%, 100%) (0%, 0%, 0%, 0%)
(75, 100%, 95%) (3%, 0%, 10%, 0%)	(75, 95%, 50%) (24%, 0%, 97%, 3%)	(75, 95%, 95%) (2%, 0%, 10%, 0%)
(75, 100%, 90%) (5%, 0%, 20%, 0%)	(75, 90%, 50%) (24%, 0%, 95%, 5%)	(75, 90%, 90%) (5%, 0%, 18%, 1%)
(75, 100%, 85%) (7%, 0%, 30%, 0%)	(75, 85%, 50%) (23%, 0%, 92%, 7%)	(75, 85%, 85%) (7%, 0%, 26%, 2%)
(75, 100%, 80%) (10%, 0%, 40%, 0%)	(75, 80%, 50%) (22%, 0%, 89%, 10%)	(75, 80%, 80%) (8%, 0%, 33%, 4%)
(75, 100%, 75%) (13%, 0%, 50%, 0%)	(75, 75%, 50%) (21%, 0%, 86%, 13%)	(75, 75%, 75%) (10%, 0%, 40%, 6%)
(75, 100%, 70%) (15%, 0%, 60%, 0%)	(75, 70%, 50%) (21%, 0%, 82%, 15%)	(75, 70%, 70%) (12%, 0%, 46%, 9%)
(75, 100%, 65%) (17%, 0%, 70%, 0%)	(75, 65%, 50%) (20%, 0%, 79%, 18%)	(75, 65%, 65%) (13%, 0%, 52%, 12%)
(75, 100%, 60%) (20%, 0%, 80%, 0%)	(75, 60%, 50%) (19%, 0%, 75%, 20%)	(75, 60%, 60%) (14%, 0%, 57%, 16%)
(75, 100%, 55%) (22%, 0%, 90%, 0%)	(75, 55%, 50%) (18%, 0%, 71%, 22%)	(75, 55%, 55%) (16%, 0%, 62%, 20%)
(75, 100%, 50%) (25%, 0%, 100%, 0%)	(75, 50%, 50%) (17%, 0%, 67%, 25%)	(75, 50%, 50%) (17%, 0%, 67%, 25%)
(75, 100%, 45%) (25%, 0%, 100%, 10%)	(75, 45%, 50%) (16%, 0%, 62%, 28%)	(75, 45%, 45%) (16%, 0%, 62%, 35%)
(75, 100%, 40%) (25%, 0%, 100%, 20%)	(75, 40%, 50%) (14%, 0%, 57%, 30%)	(75, 40%, 40%) (14%, 0%, 57%, 44%)
(75, 100%, 35%) (25%, 0%, 100%, 30%)	(75, 35%, 50%) (13%, 0%, 52%, 32%)	(75, 35%, 35%) (13%, 0%, 52%, 53%)
(75, 100%, 30%) (25%, 0%, 100%, 40%)	(75, 30%, 50%) (12%, 0%, 46%, 35%)	(75, 30%, 30%) (12%, 0%, 46%, 61%)
(75, 100%, 25%) (25%, 0%, 100%, 50%)	(75, 25%, 50%) (10%, 0%, 40%, 38%)	(75, 25%, 25%) (10%, 0%, 40%, 69%)
(75, 100%, 20%) (25%, 0%, 100%, 60%)	(75, 20%, 50%) (8%, 0%, 33%, 40%)	(75, 20%, 20%) (8%, 0%, 33%, 76%)
(75, 100%, 15%) (25%, 0%, 100%, 70%)	(75, 15%, 50%) (7%, 0%, 26%, 43%)	(75, 15%, 15%) (7%, 0%, 26%, 83%)
(75, 100%, 10%) (25%, 0%, 100%, 80%)	(75, 10%, 50%) (5%, 0%, 18%, 45%)	(75, 10%, 10%) (5%, 0%, 18%, 89%)
(75, 100%, 5%) (25%, 0%, 100%, 90%)	(75, 5%, 50%) (2%, 0%, 10%, 47%)	(75, 5%, 5%) (2%, 0%, 10%, 95%)
(75, 100%, 0%) (0%, 0%, 0%, 100%)	(75, 0%, 50%) (0%, 0%, 0%, 50%)	(75, 0%, 0%) (0%, 0%, 0%, 100%)

H = 80, S = X%, L = X%	H = 80, S = X%, L = 50%	H = 80, S = 100%, L = X%
(80, 100%, 100%) (0%, 0%, 0%, 0%)	(80, 100%, 50%) (33%, 0%, 100%, 0%)	(80, 100%, 100%) (0%, 0%, 0%, 0%)
(80, 95%, 95%) (3%, 0%, 10%, 0%)	(80, 95%, 50%) (32%, 0%, 97%, 3%)	(80, 100%, 95%) (3%, 0%, 10%, 0%)
(80, 90%, 90%) (6%, 0%, 18%, 1%)	(80, 90%, 50%) (32%, 0%, 95%, 5%)	(80, 100%, 90%) (7%, 0%, 20%, 0%)
(80, 85%, 85%) (9%, 0%, 26%, 2%)	(80, 85%, 50%) (31%, 0%, 92%, 7%)	(80, 100%, 85%) (10%, 0%, 30%, 0%)
(80, 80%, 80%) (11%, 0%, 33%, 4%)	(80, 80%, 50%) (30%, 0%, 89%, 10%)	(80, 100%, 80%) (13%, 0%, 40%, 0%)
(80, 75%, 75%) (13%, 0%, 40%, 6%)	(80, 75%, 50%) (29%, 0%, 86%, 13%)	(80, 100%, 75%) (17%, 0%, 50%, 0%)
(80, 70%, 70%) (15%, 0%, 46%, 9%)	(80, 70%, 50%) (27%, 0%, 82%, 15%)	(80, 100%, 70%) (20%, 0%, 60%, 0%)
(80, 65%, 65%) (17%, 0%, 52%, 12%)	(80, 65%, 50%) (26%, 0%, 79%, 18%)	(80, 100%, 65%) (23%, 0%, 70%, 0%)
(80, 60%, 60%) (19%, 0%, 57%, 16%)	(80, 60%, 50%) (25%, 0%, 75%, 20%)	(80, 100%, 60%) (27%, 0%, 80%, 0%)
(80, 55%, 55%) (21%, 0%, 62%, 20%)	(80, 55%, 50%) (24%, 0%, 71%, 22%)	(80, 100%, 55%) (30%, 0%, 90%, 0%)
(80, 50%, 50%) (22%, 0%, 67%, 25%)	(80, 50%, 50%) (22%, 0%, 67%, 25%)	(80, 100%, 50%) (33%, 0%, 100%, 0%)
(80, 45%, 45%) (21%, 0%, 62%, 35%)	(80, 45%, 50%) (21%, 0%, 62%, 28%)	(80, 100%, 45%) (33%, 0%, 100%, 10%)
(80, 40%, 40%) (19%, 0%, 57%, 44%)	(80, 40%, 50%) (19%, 0%, 57%, 30%)	(80, 100%, 40%) (33%, 0%, 100%, 20%)
(80, 35%, 35%) (17%, 0%, 52%, 53%)	(80, 35%, 50%) (17%, 0%, 52%, 32%)	(80, 100%, 35%) (33%, 0%, 100%, 30%)
(80, 30%, 30%) (15%, 0%, 46%, 61%)	(80, 30%, 50%) (15%, 0%, 46%, 35%)	(80, 100%, 30%) (33%, 0%, 100%, 40%)
(80, 25%, 25%) (13%, 0%, 40%, 69%)	(80, 25%, 50%) (13%, 0%, 40%, 38%)	(80, 100%, 25%) (33%, 0%, 100%, 50%)
(80, 20%, 20%) (11%, 0%, 33%, 76%)	(80, 20%, 50%) (11%, 0%, 33%, 40%)	(80, 100%, 20%) (33%, 0%, 100%, 60%)
(80, 15%, 15%) (9%, 0%, 26%, 83%)	(80, 15%, 50%) (9%, 0%, 26%, 43%)	(80, 100%, 15%) (33%, 0%, 100%, 70%)
(80, 10%, 10%) (6%, 0%, 18%, 89%)	(80, 10%, 50%) (6%, 0%, 18%, 45%)	(80, 100%, 10%) (33%, 0%, 100%, 80%)
(80, 5%, 5%) (3%, 0%, 10%, 95%)	(80, 5%, 50%) (3%, 0%, 10%, 47%)	(80, 100%, 5%) (33%, 0%, 100%, 90%)
(80, 0%, 0%) (0%, 0%, 0%, 100%)	(80, 0%, 50%) (0%, 0%, 0%, 50%)	(80, 100%, 0%) (0%, 0%, 0%, 100%)

H = 85, S = 100%, L = X%	H = 85, S = X%, L = 50%	H = 85, S = X%, L = X%
(85, 100%, 100%) (0%, 0%, 0%, 0%)	(85, 100%, 50%) (42%, 0%, 100%, 0%)	(85, 100%, 100%) (0%, 0%, 0%, 0%)
(85, 100%, 95%) (4%, 0%, 10%, 0%)	(85, 95%, 50%) (41%, 0%, 97%, 3%)	(85, 95%, 95%) (4%, 0%, 10%, 0%)
(85, 100%, 90%) (8%, 0%, 20%, 0%)	(85, 90%, 50%) (39%, 0%, 95%, 5%)	(85, 90%, 90%) (8%, 0%, 18%, 1%)
(85, 100%, 85%) (13%, 0%, 30%, 0%)	(85, 85%, 50%) (38%, 0%, 92%, 7%)	(85, 85%, 85%) (11%, 0%, 26%, 2%)
(85, 100%, 80%) (17%, 0%, 40%, 0%)	(85, 80%, 50%) (37%, 0%, 89%, 10%)	(85, 80%, 80%) (14%, 0%, 33%, 4%)
(85, 100%, 75%) (21%, 0%, 50%, 0%)	(85, 75%, 50%) (36%, 0%, 86%, 13%)	(85, 75%, 75%) (17%, 0%, 40%, 6%)
(85, 100%, 70%) (25%, 0%, 60%, 0%)	(85, 70%, 50%) (34%, 0%, 82%, 15%)	(85, 70%, 70%) (19%, 0%, 46%, 9%)
(85, 100%, 65%) (29%, 0%, 70%, 0%)	(85, 65%, 50%) (33%, 0%, 79%, 18%)	(85, 65%, 65%) (22%, 0%, 52%, 12%)
(85, 100%, 60%) (33%, 0%, 80%, 0%)	(85, 60%, 50%) (31%, 0%, 75%, 20%)	(85, 60%, 60%) (24%, 0%, 57%, 16%)
(85, 100%, 55%) (38%, 0%, 90%, 0%)	(85, 55%, 50%) (30%, 0%, 71%, 22%)	(85, 55%, 55%) (26%, 0%, 62%, 20%)
(85, 100%, 50%) (42%, 0%, 100%, 0%)	(85, 50%, 50%) (28%, 0%, 67%, 25%)	(85, 50%, 50%) (28%, 0%, 67%, 25%)
(85, 100%, 45%) (42%, 0%, 100%, 10%)	(85, 45%, 50%) (26%, 0%, 62%, 28%)	(85, 45%, 45%) (26%, 0%, 62%, 35%)
(85, 100%, 40%) (42%, 0%, 100%, 20%)	(85, 40%, 50%) (24%, 0%, 57%, 30%)	(85, 40%, 40%) (24%, 0%, 57%, 44%)
(85, 100%, 35%) (42%, 0%, 100%, 30%)	(85, 35%, 50%) (22%, 0%, 52%, 32%)	(85, 35%, 35%) (22%, 0%, 52%, 53%)
(85, 100%, 30%) (42%, 0%, 100%, 40%)	(85, 30%, 50%) (19%, 0%, 46%, 35%)	(85, 30%, 30%) (19%, 0%, 46%, 61%)
(85, 100%, 25%) (42%, 0%, 100%, 50%)	(85, 25%, 50%) (17%, 0%, 40%, 38%)	(85, 25%, 25%) (17%, 0%, 40%, 69%)
(85, 100%, 20%) (42%, 0%, 100%, 60%)	(85, 20%, 50%) (14%, 0%, 33%, 40%)	(85, 20%, 20%) (14%, 0%, 33%, 76%)
(85, 100%, 15%) (42%, 0%, 100%, 70%)	(85, 15%, 50%) (11%, 0%, 26%, 43%)	(85, 15%, 15%) (11%, 0%, 26%, 83%)
(85, 100%, 10%) (42%, 0%, 100%, 80%)	(85, 10%, 50%) (8%, 0%, 18%, 45%)	(85, 10%, 10%) (8%, 0%, 18%, 89%)
(85, 100%, 5%) (42%, 0%, 100%, 90%)	(85, 5%, 50%) (4%, 0%, 10%, 47%)	(85, 5%, 5%) (4%, 0%, 10%, 95%)
(85, 100%, 0%) (0%, 0%, 0%, 100%)	(85, 0%, 50%) (0%, 0%, 0%, 50%)	(85, 0%, 0%) (0%, 0%, 0%, 100%)

H = 90, S = X%, L = X%	H = 90, S = X%, L = 50%	H = 90, S = 100%, L = X%
(90, 100%, 100%) (0%, 0%, 0%, 0%)	(90, 100%, 50%) (50%, 0%, 100%, 0%)	(90, 100%, 100%) (0%, 0%, 0%, 0%)
(90, 95%, 95%) (5%, 0%, 10%, 0%)	(90, 95%, 50%) (49%, 0%, 97%, 3%)	(90, 100%, 95%) (5%, 0%, 10%, 0%)
(90, 90%, 90%) (9%, 0%, 18%, 1%)	(90, 90%, 50%) (47%, 0%, 95%, 5%)	(90, 100%, 90%) (10%, 0%, 20%, 0%)
(90, 85%, 85%) (13%, 0%, 26%, 2%)	(90, 85%, 50%) (46%, 0%, 92%, 7%)	(90, 100%, 85%) (15%, 0%, 30%, 0%)
(90, 80%, 80%) (17%, 0%, 33%, 4%)	(90, 80%, 50%) (44%, 0%, 89%, 10%)	(90, 100%, 80%) (20%, 0%, 40%, 0%)
(90, 75%, 75%) (20%, 0%, 40%, 6%)	(90, 75%, 50%) (43%, 0%, 86%, 13%)	(90, 100%, 75%) (25%, 0%, 50%, 0%)
(90, 70%, 70%) (23%, 0%, 46%, 9%)	(90, 70%, 50%) (41%, 0%, 82%, 15%)	(90, 100%, 70%) (30%, 0%, 60%, 0%)
(90, 65%, 65%) (26%, 0%, 52%, 12%)	(90, 65%, 50%) (39%, 0%, 79%, 18%)	(90, 100%, 65%) (35%, 0%, 70%, 0%)
(90, 60%, 60%) (29%, 0%, 57%, 16%)	(90, 60%, 50%) (38%, 0%, 75%, 20%)	(90, 100%, 60%) (40%, 0%, 80%, 0%)
(90, 55%, 55%) (31%, 0%, 62%, 20%)	(90, 55%, 50%) (35%, 0%, 71%, 22%)	(90, 100%, 55%) (45%, 0%, 90%, 0%)
(90, 50%, 50%) (33%, 0%, 67%, 25%)	(90, 50%, 50%) (33%, 0%, 67%, 25%)	(90, 100%, 50%) (50%, 0%, 100%, 0%)
(90, 45%, 45%) (31%, 0%, 62%, 35%)	(90, 45%, 50%) (31%, 0%, 62%, 28%)	(90, 100%, 45%) (50%, 0%, 100%, 10%)
(90, 40%, 40%) (29%, 0%, 57%, 44%)	(90, 40%, 50%) (29%, 0%, 57%, 30%)	(90, 100%, 40%) (50%, 0%, 100%, 20%)
(90, 35%, 35%) (26%, 0%, 52%, 53%)	(90, 35%, 50%) (26%, 0%, 52%, 32%)	(90, 100%, 35%) (50%, 0%, 100%, 30%)
(90, 30%, 30%) (23%, 0%, 46%, 61%)	(90, 30%, 50%) (23%, 0%, 46%, 35%)	(90, 100%, 30%) (50%, 0%, 100%, 40%)
(90, 25%, 25%) (20%, 0%, 40%, 69%)	(90, 25%, 50%) (20%, 0%, 40%, 38%)	(90, 100%, 25%) (50%, 0%, 100%, 50%)
(90, 20%, 20%) (17%, 0%, 33%, 76%)	(90, 20%, 50%) (17%, 0%, 33%, 40%)	(90, 100%, 20%) (50%, 0%, 100%, 60%)
(90, 15%, 15%) (13%, 0%, 26%, 83%)	(90, 15%, 50%) (13%, 0%, 26%, 43%)	(90, 100%, 15%) (50%, 0%, 100%, 70%)
(90, 10%, 10%) (9%, 0%, 18%, 89%)	(90, 10%, 50%) (9%, 0%, 18%, 45%)	(90, 100%, 10%) (50%, 0%, 100%, 80%)
(90, 5%, 5%) (5%, 0%, 10%, 95%)	(90, 5%, 50%) (5%, 0%, 10%, 47%)	(90, 100%, 5%) (50%, 0%, 100%, 90%)
(90, 0%, 0%) (0%, 0%, 0%, 100%)	(90, 0%, 50%) (0%, 0%, 0%, 50%)	(90, 100%, 0%) (0%, 0%, 0%, 100%)

H = 95, S = 100%, L = X%	H = 95, S = X%, L = 50%	H = 95, S = X%, L = X%
(95, 100%, 100%) (0%, 0%, 0%, 0%)	(95, 100%, 50%) (58%, 0%, 100%, 0%)	(95, 100%, 100%) (0%, 0%, 0%, 0%)
(95, 100%, 95%) (6%, 0%, 10%, 0%)	(95, 95%, 50%) (57%, 0%, 97%, 3%)	(95, 95%, 95%) (6%, 0%, 10%, 0%)
(95, 100%, 90%) (12%, 0%, 20%, 0%)	(95, 90%, 50%) (55%, 0%, 95%, 5%)	(95, 90%, 90%) (11%, 0%, 18%, 1%)
(95, 100%, 85%) (17%, 0%, 30%, 0%)	(95, 85%, 50%) (54%, 0%, 92%, 7%)	(95, 85%, 85%) (15%, 0%, 26%, 2%)
(95, 100%, 80%) (23%, 0%, 40%, 0%)	(95, 80%, 50%) (52%, 0%, 89%, 10%)	(95, 80%, 80%) (19%, 0%, 33%, 4%)
(95, 100%, 75%) (29%, 0%, 50%, 0%)	(95, 75%, 50%) (50%, 0%, 86%, 13%)	(95, 75%, 75%) (23%, 0%, 40%, 6%)
(95, 100%, 70%) (35%, 0%, 60%, 0%)	(95, 70%, 50%) (48%, 0%, 82%, 15%)	(95, 70%, 70%) (27%, 0%, 46%, 9%)
(95, 100%, 65%) (41%, 0%, 70%, 0%)	(95, 65%, 50%) (46%, 0%, 79%, 18%)	(95, 65%, 65%) (30%, 0%, 52%, 12%)
(95, 100%, 60%) (47%, 0%, 80%, 0%)	(95, 60%, 50%) (44%, 0%, 75%, 20%)	(95, 60%, 60%) (33%, 0%, 57%, 16%)
(95, 100%, 55%) (52%, 0%, 90%, 0%)	(95, 55%, 50%) (41%, 0%, 71%, 22%)	(95, 55%, 55%) (36%, 0%, 62%, 20%)
(95, 100%, 50%) (58%, 0%, 100%, 0%)	(95, 50%, 50%) (39%, 0%, 67%, 25%)	(95, 50%, 50%) (39%, 0%, 67%, 25%)
(95, 100%, 45%) (58%, 0%, 100%, 10%)	(95, 45%, 50%) (36%, 0%, 62%, 28%)	(95, 45%, 45%) (36%, 0%, 62%, 35%)
(95, 100%, 40%) (58%, 0%, 100%, 20%)	(95, 40%, 50%) (33%, 0%, 57%, 30%)	(95, 40%, 40%) (33%, 0%, 57%, 44%)
(95, 100%, 35%) (58%, 0%, 100%, 30%)	(95, 35%, 50%) (35%, 0%, 52%, 32%)	(95, 35%, 35%) (30%, 0%, 52%, 53%)
(95, 100%, 30%) (58%, 0%, 100%, 40%)	(95, 30%, 50%) (27%, 0%, 46%, 35%)	(95, 30%, 30%) (27%, 0%, 46%, 61%)
(95, 100%, 25%) (58%, 0%, 100%, 50%)	(95, 25%, 50%) (23%, 0%, 40%, 38%)	(95, 25%, 25%) (23%, 0%, 40%, 69%)
(95, 100%, 20%) (58%, 0%, 100%, 60%)	(95, 20%, 50%) (19%, 0%, 33%, 40%)	(95, 20%, 20%) (19%, 0%, 33%, 76%)
(95, 100%, 15%) (58%, 0%, 100%, 70%)	(95, 15%, 50%) (15%, 0%, 26%, 43%)	(95, 15%, 15%) (15%, 0%, 26%, 83%)
(95, 100%, 10%) (58%, 0%, 100%, 80%)	(95, 10%, 50%) (11%, 0%, 18%, 45%)	(95, 10%, 10%) (11%, 0%, 18%, 89%)
(95, 100%, 5%) (58%, 0%, 100%, 90%)	(95, 5%, 50%) (6%, 0%, 10%, 47%)	(95, 5%, 5%) (6%, 0%, 10%, 95%)
(95, 100%, 0%) (0%, 0%, 0%, 100%)	(95, 0%, 50%) (0%, 0%, 0%, 50%)	(95, 0%, 0%) (0%, 0%, 0%, 100%)

H = 100, S = X%, L = X%	H = 100, S = X%, L = 50%	H = 100, S = 100%, L = X%
(100, 100%, 100%) (0%, 0%, 0%, 0%)	(100, 100%, 50%) (67%, 0%, 100%, 0%)	(100, 100%, 100%) (0%, 0%, 0%, 0%)
(100, 95%, 95%) (6%, 0%, 10%, 0%)	(100, 95%, 50%) (65%, 0%, 97%, 3%)	(100, 100%, 95%) (7%, 0%, 10%, 0%)
(100, 90%, 90%) (12%, 0%, 18%, 1%)	(100, 90%, 50%) (63%, 0%, 95%, 5%)	(100, 100%, 90%) (13%, 0%, 20%, 0%)
(100, 85%, 85%) (17%, 0%, 26%, 2%)	(100, 85%, 50%) (61%, 0%, 92%, 7%)	(100, 100%, 85%) (20%, 0%, 30%, 0%)
(100, 80%, 80%) (22%, 0%, 33%, 4%)	(100, 80%, 50%) (59%, 0%, 89%, 10%)	(100, 100%, 80%) (27%, 0%, 40%, 0%)
(100, 75%, 75%) (27%, 0%, 40%, 6%)	(100, 75%, 50%) (57%, 0%, 86%, 13%)	(100, 100%, 75%) (33%, 0%, 50%, 0%)
(100, 70%, 70%) (31%, 0%, 46%, 9%)	(100, 70%, 50%) (55%, 0%, 82%, 15%)	(100, 100%, 70%) (40%, 0%, 60%, 0%)
(100, 65%, 65%) (35%, 0%, 52%, 12%)	(100, 65%, 50%) (53%, 0%, 79%, 18%)	(100, 100%, 65%) (47%, 0%, 70%, 0%)
(100, 60%, 60%) (38%, 0%, 57%, 16%)	(100, 60%, 50%) (50%, 0%, 75%, 20%)	(100, 100%, 60%) (53%, 0%, 80%, 0%)
(100, 55%, 55%) (41%, 0%, 62%, 20%)	(100, 55%, 50%) (47%, 0%, 71%, 22%)	(100, 100%, 55%) (60%, 0%, 90%, 0%)
(100, 50%, 50%) (44%, 0%, 67%, 25%)	(100, 50%, 50%) (44%, 0%, 67%, 25%)	(100, 100%, 50%) (67%, 0%, 100%, 0%)
(100, 45%, 45%) (41%, 0%, 62%, 35%)	(100, 45%, 50%) (41%, 0%, 62%, 28%)	(100, 100%, 45%) (67%, 0%, 100%, 10%)
(100, 40%, 40%) (38%, 0%, 57%, 44%)	(100, 40%, 50%) (38%, 0%, 57%, 30%)	(100, 100%, 40%) (67%, 0%, 100%, 20%)
(100, 35%, 35%) (35%, 0%, 52%, 53%)	(100, 35%, 50%) (35%, 0%, 52%, 32%)	(100, 100%, 35%) (67%, 0%, 100%, 30%)
(100, 30%, 30%) (31%, 0%, 46%, 61%)	(100, 30%, 50%) (31%, 0%, 46%, 35%)	(100, 100%, 30%) (67%, 0%, 100%, 40%)
(100, 25%, 25%) (27%, 0%, 40%, 69%)	(100, 25%, 50%) (27%, 0%, 40%, 38%)	(100, 100%, 25%) (67%, 0%, 100%, 50%)
(100, 20%, 20%) (22%, 0%, 33%, 76%)	(100, 20%, 50%) (22%, 0%, 33%, 40%)	(100, 100%, 20%) (67%, 0%, 100%, 60%)
(100, 15%, 15%) (17%, 0%, 26%, 83%)	(100, 15%, 50%) (17%, 0%, 26%, 43%)	(100, 100%, 15%) (67%, 0%, 100%, 70%)
(100, 10%, 10%) (12%, 0%, 18%, 89%)	(100, 10%, 50%) (12%, 0%, 18%, 45%)	(100, 100%, 10%) (67%, 0%, 100%, 80%)
(100, 5%, 5%) (6%, 0%, 10%, 95%)	(100, 5%, 50%) (6%, 0%, 10%, 47%)	(100, 100%, 5%) (67%, 0%, 100%, 90%)
(100, 0%, 0%) (0%, 0%, 0%, 100%)	(100, 0%, 50%) (0%, 0%, 0%, 50%)	(100, 100%, 0%) (0%, 0%, 0%, 100%)

H = 105, S = 100%, L = X%	H = 105, S = X%, L = 50%	H = 105, S = X%, L = X%
(105, 100%, 100%) (0%, 0%, 0%, 0%)	(105, 100%, 50%) (75%, 0%, 100%, 0%)	(105, 100%, 100%) (0%, 0%, 0%, 0%)
(105, 100%, 95%) (8%, 0%, 10%, 0%)	(105, 95%, 50%) (73%, 0%, 97%, 3%)	(105, 95%, 95%) (7%, 0%, 10%, 0%)
(105, 100%, 90%) (15%, 0%, 20%, 0%)	(105, 90%, 50%) (71%, 0%, 95%, 5%)	(105, 90%, 90%) (14%, 0%, 18%, 1%)
(105, 100%, 85%) (23%, 0%, 30%, 0%)	(105, 85%, 50%) (69%, 0%, 92%, 7%)	(105, 85%, 85%) (20%, 0%, 26%, 2%)
(105, 100%, 80%) (30%, 0%, 40%, 0%)	(105, 80%, 50%) (67%, 0%, 89%, 10%)	(105, 80%, 80%) (25%, 0%, 33%, 4%)
(105, 100%, 75%) (38%, 0%, 50%, 0%)	(105, 75%, 50%) (64%, 0%, 86%, 13%)	(105, 75%, 75%) (30%, 0%, 40%, 6%)
(105, 100%, 70%) (45%, 0%, 60%, 0%)	(105, 70%, 50%) (62%, 0%, 82%, 15%)	(105, 70%, 70%) (35%, 0%, 46%, 9%)
(105, 100%, 65%) (52%, 0%, 70%, 0%)	(105, 65%, 50%) (59%, 0%, 79%, 18%)	(105, 65%, 65%) (39%, 0%, 52%, 12%)
(105, 100%, 60%) (60%, 0%, 80%, 0%)	(105, 60%, 50%) (56%, 0%, 75%, 20%)	(105, 60%, 60%) (43%, 0%, 57%, 16%)
(105, 100%, 55%) (67%, 0%, 90%, 0%)	(105, 55%, 50%) (53%, 0%, 71%, 22%)	(105, 55%, 55%) (47%, 0%, 62%, 20%)
(105, 100%, 50%) (75%, 0%, 100%, 0%)	(105, 50%, 50%) (50%, 0%, 67%, 25%)	(105, 50%, 50%) (50%, 0%, 67%, 25%)
(105, 100%, 45%) (75%, 0%, 100%, 10%)	(105, 45%, 50%) (47%, 0%, 62%, 28%)	(105, 45%, 45%) (47%, 0%, 62%, 35%)
(105, 100%, 40%) (75%, 0%, 100%, 20%)	(105, 40%, 50%) (43%, 0%, 57%, 30%)	(105, 40%, 40%) (43%, 0%, 57%, 44%)
(105, 100%, 35%) (75%, 0%, 100%, 30%)	(105, 35%, 50%) (39%, 0%, 52%, 32%)	(105, 35%, 35%) (39%, 0%, 52%, 53%)
(105, 100%, 30%) (75%, 0%, 100%, 40%)	(105, 30%, 50%) (35%, 0%, 46%, 35%)	(105, 30%, 30%) (35%, 0%, 46%, 61%)
(105, 100%, 25%) (75%, 0%, 100%, 50%)	(105, 25%, 50%) (30%, 0%, 40%, 38%)	(105, 25%, 25%) (30%, 0%, 40%, 69%)
(105, 100%, 20%) (75%, 0%, 100%, 60%)	(105, 20%, 50%) (25%, 0%, 33%, 40%)	(105, 20%, 20%) (25%, 0%, 33%, 76%)
(105, 100%, 15%) (75%, 0%, 100%, 70%)	(105, 15%, 50%) (20%, 0%, 26%, 43%)	(105, 15%, 15%) (20%, 0%, 26%, 83%)
(105, 100%, 10%) (75%, 0%, 100%, 80%)	(105, 10%, 50%) (14%, 0%, 18%, 45%)	(105, 10%, 10%) (14%, 0%, 18%, 89%)
(105, 100%, 5%) (75%, 0%, 100%, 90%)	(105, 5%, 50%) (7%, 0%, 10%, 47%)	(105, 5%, 5%) (7%, 0%, 10%, 95%)
(105, 100%, 0%) (0%, 0%, 0%, 100%)	(105, 0%, 50%) (0%, 0%, 0%, 50%)	(105, 0%, 0%) (0%, 0%, 0%, 100%)

H = 110, S = X%, L = X%	H = 110, S = X%, L = 50%	H = 110, S = 100%, L = X%
(110, 100%, 100%) (0%, 0%, 0%, 0%)	(110, 100%, 50%) (83%, 0%, 100%, 0%)	(110, 100%, 100%) (0%, 0%, 0%, 0%)
(110, 95%, 95%) (8%, 0%, 10%, 0%)	(110, 95%, 50%) (81%, 0%, 97%, 3%)	(110, 100%, 95%) (8%, 0%, 10%, 0%)
(110, 90%, 90%) (15%, 0%, 18%, 1%)	(110, 90%, 50%) (79%, 0%, 95%, 5%)	(110, 100%, 90%) (17%, 0%, 20%, 0%)
(110, 85%, 85%) (22%, 0%, 26%, 2%)	(110, 85%, 50%) (77%, 0%, 92%, 7%)	(110, 100%, 85%) (25%, 0%, 30%, 0%)
(110, 80%, 80%) (28%, 0%, 33%, 4%)	(110, 80%, 50%) (74%, 0%, 89%, 10%)	(110, 100%, 80%) (33%, 0%, 40%, 0%)
(110, 75%, 75%) (33%, 0%, 40%, 6%)	(110, 75%, 50%) (71%, 0%, 86%, 13%)	(110, 100%, 75%) (42%, 0%, 50%, 0%)
(110, 70%, 70%) (38%, 0%, 46%, 9%)	(110, 70%, 50%) (69%, 0%, 82%, 15%)	(110, 100%, 70%) (50%, 0%, 60%, 0%)
(110, 65%, 65%) (43%, 0%, 52%, 12%)	(110, 65%, 50%) (66%, 0%, 79%, 18%)	(110, 100%, 65%) (58%, 0%, 70%, 0%)
(110, 60%, 60%) (48%, 0%, 57%, 16%)	(110, 60%, 50%) (62%, 0%, 75%, 20%)	(110, 100%, 60%) (67%, 0%, 80%, 0%)
(110, 55%, 55%) (52%, 0%, 62%, 20%)	(110, 55%, 50%) (59%, 0%, 71%, 22%)	(110, 100%, 55%) (75%, 0%, 90%, 0%)
(110, 50%, 50%) (56%, 0%, 67%, 25%)	(110, 50%, 50%) (56%, 0%, 67%, 25%)	(110, 100%, 50%) (83%, 0%, 100%, 0%)
(110, 45%, 45%) (52%, 0%, 62%, 35%)	(110, 45%, 50%) (52%, 0%, 62%, 28%)	(110, 100%, 45%) (83%, 0%, 100%, 10%)
(110, 40%, 40%) (48%, 0%, 57%, 44%)	(110, 40%, 50%) (48%, 0%, 57%, 30%)	(110, 100%, 40%) (83%, 0%, 100%, 20%)
(110, 35%, 35%) (43%, 0%, 52%, 53%)	(110, 35%, 50%) (43%, 0%, 52%, 32%)	(110, 100%, 35%) (83%, 0%, 100%, 30%)
(110, 30%, 30%) (38%, 0%, 46%, 61%)	(110, 30%, 50%) (38%, 0%, 46%, 35%)	(110, 100%, 30%) (83%, 0%, 100%, 40%)
(110, 25%, 25%) (33%, 0%, 40%, 69%)	(110, 25%, 50%) (33%, 0%, 40%, 38%)	(110, 100%, 25%) (83%, 0%, 100%, 50%)
(110, 20%, 20%) (28%, 0%, 33%, 76%)	(110, 20%, 50%) (28%, 0%, 33%, 40%)	(110, 100%, 20%) (83%, 0%, 100%, 60%)
(110, 15%, 15%) (22%, 0%, 26%, 83%)	(110, 15%, 50%) (22%, 0%, 26%, 43%)	(110, 100%, 15%) (83%, 0%, 100%, 70%)
(110, 10%, 10%) (15%, 0%, 18%, 89%)	(110, 10%, 50%) (15%, 0%, 18%, 45%)	(110, 100%, 10%) (83%, 0%, 100%, 80%)
(110, 5%, 5%) (8%, 0%, 10%, 95%)	(110, 5%, 50%) (8%, 0%, 10%, 47%)	(110, 100%, 5%) (83%, 0%, 100%, 90%)
(110, 0%, 0%) (0%, 0%, 0%, 100%)	(110, 0%, 50%) (0%, 0%, 0%, 50%)	(110, 100%, 0%) (0%, 0%, 0%, 100%)

H = 115, S = 100%, L = X%	H = 115, S = X%, L = 50%	H = 115, S = X%, L = X%
(115, 100%, 100%) (0%, 0%, 0%, 0%)	(115, 100%, 50%) (92%, 0%, 100%, 0%)	(115, 100%, 100%) (0%, 0%, 0%, 0%)
(115, 100%, 95%) (9%, 0%, 10%, 0%)	(115, 95%, 50%) (89%, 0%, 97%, 3%)	(115, 95%, 95%) (9%, 0%, 10%, 0%)
(115, 100%, 90%) (18%, 0%, 20%, 0%)	(115, 90%, 50%) (87%, 0%, 95%, 5%)	(115, 90%, 90%) (17%, 0%, 18%, 1%)
(115, 100%, 85%) (28%, 0%, 30%, 0%)	(115, 85%, 50%) (84%, 0%, 92%, 7%)	(115, 85%, 85%) (24%, 0%, 26%, 2%)
(115, 100%, 80%) (37%, 0%, 40%, 0%)	(115, 80%, 50%) (81%, 0%, 89%, 10%)	(115, 80%, 80%) (31%, 0%, 33%, 4%)
(115, 100%, 75%) (46%, 0%, 50%, 0%)	(115, 75%, 50%) (79%, 0%, 86%, 13%)	(115, 75%, 75%) (37%, 0%, 40%, 6%)
(115, 100%, 70%) (55%, 0%, 60%, 0%)	(115, 70%, 50%) (75%, 0%, 82%, 15%)	(115, 70%, 70%) (42%, 0%, 46%, 9%)
(115, 100%, 65%) (64%, 0%, 70%, 0%)	(115, 65%, 50%) (72%, 0%, 79%, 18%)	(115, 65%, 65%) (48%, 0%, 52%, 12%)
(115, 100%, 60%) (73%, 0%, 80%, 0%)	(115, 60%, 50%) (69%, 0%, 75%, 20%)	(115, 60%, 60%) (52%, 0%, 57%, 16%)
(115, 100%, 55%) (83%, 0%, 90%, 0%)	(115, 55%, 50%) (65%, 0%, 71%, 22%)	(115, 55%, 55%) (57%, 0%, 62%, 20%)
(115, 100%, 50%) (92%, 0%, 100%, 0%)	(115, 50%, 50%) (61%, 0%, 67%, 25%)	(115, 50%, 50%) (61%, 0%, 67%, 25%)
(115, 100%, 45%) (92%, 0%, 100%, 10%)	(115, 45%, 50%) (57%, 0%, 62%, 28%)	(115, 45%, 45%) (57%, 0%, 62%, 35%)
(115, 100%, 40%) (92%, 0%, 100%, 20%)	(115, 40%, 50%) (52%, 0%, 57%, 30%)	(115, 40%, 40%) (52%, 0%, 57%, 44%)
(115, 100%, 35%) (92%, 0%, 100%, 30%)	(115, 35%, 50%) (48%, 0%, 52%, 32%)	(115, 35%, 35%) (48%, 0%, 52%, 53%)
(115, 100%, 30%) (92%, 0%, 100%, 40%)	(115, 30%, 50%) (42%, 0%, 46%, 35%)	(115, 30%, 30%) (42%, 0%, 46%, 61%)
(115, 100%, 25%) (92%, 0%, 100%, 50%)	(115, 25%, 50%) (37%, 0%, 40%, 38%)	(115, 25%, 25%) (37%, 0%, 40%, 69%)
(115, 100%, 20%) (92%, 0%, 100%, 60%)	(115, 20%, 50%) (31%, 0%, 33%, 40%)	(115, 20%, 20%) (31%, 0%, 33%, 76%)
(115, 100%, 15%) (92%, 0%, 100%, 70%)	(115, 15%, 50%) (24%, 0%, 26%, 43%)	(115, 15%, 15%) (24%, 0%, 26%, 83%)
(115, 100%, 10%) (92%, 0%, 100%, 80%)	(115, 10%, 50%) (17%, 0%, 18%, 45%)	(115, 10%, 10%) (17%, 0%, 18%, 89%)
(115, 100%, 5%) (92%, 0%, 100%, 90%)	(115, 5%, 50%) (9%, 0%, 10%, 47%)	(115, 5%, 5%) (9%, 0%, 10%, 95%)
(115, 100%, 0%) (0%, 0%, 0%, 100%)	(115, 0%, 50%) (0%, 0%, 0%, 50%)	(115, 0%, 0%) (0%, 0%, 0%, 100%)

H = 120, S = X%, L = X%	H = 120, S = X%, L = 50%	H = 120, S = 100%, L = X%
(120, 100%, 100%) (0%, 0%, 0%, 0%)	(120, 100%, 50%) (100%, 0%, 100%, 0%)	(120, 100%, 100%) (0%, 0%, 0%, 0%)
(120, 95%, 95%) (10%, 0%, 10%, 0%)	(120, 95%, 50%) (97%, 0%, 97%, 3%)	(120, 100%, 95%) (10%, 0%, 10%, 0%)
(120, 90%, 90%) (18%, 0%, 18%, 1%)	(120, 90%, 50%) (95%, 0%, 95%, 5%)	(120, 100%, 90%) (20%, 0%, 20%, 0%)
(120, 85%, 85%) (26%, 0%, 26%, 2%)	(120, 85%, 50%) (92%, 0%, 92%, 7%)	(120, 100%, 85%) (30%, 0%, 30%, 0%)
(120, 80%, 80%) (33%, 0%, 33%, 4%)	(120, 80%, 50%) (89%, 0%, 89%, 10%)	(120, 100%, 80%) (40%, 0%, 40%, 0%)
(120, 75%, 75%) (40%, 0%, 40%, 6%)	(120, 75%, 50%) (86%, 0%, 86%, 13%)	(120, 100%, 75%) (50%, 0%, 50%, 0%)
(120, 70%, 70%) (46%, 0%, 46%, 9%)	(120, 70%, 50%) (82%, 0%, 82%, 15%)	(120, 100%, 70%) (60%, 0%, 60%, 0%)
(120, 65%, 65%) (52%, 0%, 52%, 12%)	(120, 65%, 50%) (79%, 0%, 79%, 18%)	(120, 100%, 65%) (70%, 0%, 70%, 0%)
(120, 60%, 60%) (57%, 0%, 57%, 16%)	(120, 60%, 50%) (75%, 0%, 75%, 20%)	(120, 100%, 60%) (80%, 0%, 80%, 0%)
(120, 55%, 55%) (62%, 0%, 62%, 20%)	(120, 55%, 50%) (71%, 0%, 71%, 22%)	(120, 100%, 55%) (90%, 0%, 90%, 0%)
(120, 50%, 50%) (67%, 0%, 67%, 25%)	(120, 50%, 50%) (67%, 0%, 67%, 25%)	(120, 100%, 50%) (100%, 0%, 100%, 0%)
(120, 45%, 45%) (62%, 0%, 62%, 35%)	(120, 45%, 50%) (62%, 0%, 62%, 28%)	(120, 100%, 45%) (100%, 0%, 100%, 10%)
(120, 40%, 40%) (57%, 0%, 57%, 44%)	(120, 40%, 50%) (57%, 0%, 57%, 30%)	(120, 100%, 40%) (100%, 0%, 100%, 20%)
(120, 35%, 35%) (52%, 0%, 52%, 53%)	(120, 35%, 50%) (52%, 0%, 52%, 32%)	(120, 100%, 35%) (100%, 0%, 100%, 30%)
(120, 30%, 30%) (46%, 0%, 46%, 61%)	(120, 30%, 50%) (46%, 0%, 46%, 35%)	(120, 100%, 30%) (100%, 0%, 100%, 40%)
(120, 25%, 25%) (40%, 0%, 40%, 69%)	(120, 25%, 50%) (40%, 0%, 40%, 38%)	(120, 100%, 25%) (100%, 0%, 100%, 50%)
(120, 20%, 20%) (33%, 0%, 33%, 76%)	(120, 20%, 50%) (33%, 0%, 33%, 40%)	(120, 100%, 20%) (100%, 0%, 100%, 60%)
(120, 15%, 15%) (26%, 0%, 26%, 83%)	(120, 15%, 50%) (26%, 0%, 26%, 43%)	(120, 100%, 15%) (100%, 0%, 100%, 70%)
(120, 10%, 10%) (18%, 0%, 18%, 89%)	(120, 10%, 50%) (18%, 0%, 18%, 45%)	(120, 100%, 10%) (100%, 0%, 100%, 80%)
(120, 5%, 5%) (10%, 0%, 10%, 95%)	(120, 5%, 50%) (10%, 0%, 10%, 47%)	(120, 100%, 5%) (100%, 0%, 100%, 90%)
(120, 0%, 0%) (0%, 0%, 0%, 100%)	(120, 0%, 50%) (0%, 0%, 0%, 50%)	(120, 100%, 0%) (0%, 0%, 0%, 100%)

H = 125, S = 100%, L = X%	H = 125, S = X%, L = 50%	H = 125, S = X%, L = X%
(125, 100%, 100%) (0%, 0%, 0%, 0%)	(125, 100%, 50%) (100%, 0%, 92%, 0%)	(125, 100%, 100%) (0%, 0%, 0%, 0%)
(125, 100%, 95%) (10%, 0%, 9%, 0%)	(125, 95%, 50%) (97%, 0%, 89%, 3%)	(125, 95%, 95%) (10%, 0%, 9%, 0%)
(125, 100%, 90%) (20%, 0%, 18%, 0%)	(125, 90%, 50%) (95%, 0%, 87%, 5%)	(125, 90%, 90%) (18%, 0%, 17%, 1%)
(125, 100%, 85%) (30%, 0%, 28%, 0%)	(125, 85%, 50%) (92%, 0%, 84%, 7%)	(125, 85%, 85%) (26%, 0%, 24%, 2%)
(125, 100%, 80%) (40%, 0%, 37%, 0%)	(125, 80%, 50%) (89%, 0%, 81%, 10%)	(125, 80%, 80%) (33%, 0%, 31%, 4%)
(125, 100%, 75%) (50%, 0%, 46%, 0%)	(125, 75%, 50%) (86%, 0%, 79%, 13%)	(125, 75%, 75%) (40%, 0%, 37%, 6%)
(125, 100%, 70%) (60%, 0%, 55%, 0%)	(125, 70%, 50%) (82%, 0%, 75%, 15%)	(125, 70%, 70%) (46%, 0%, 42%, 9%)
(125, 100%, 65%) (70%, 0%, 64%, 0%)	(125, 65%, 50%) (79%, 0%, 72%, 18%)	(125, 65%, 65%) (52%, 0%, 48%, 12%)
(125, 100%, 60%) (80%, 0%, 73%, 0%)	(125, 60%, 50%) (75%, 0%, 69%, 20%)	(125, 60%, 60%) (57%, 0%, 52%, 16%)
(125, 100%, 55%) (90%, 0%, 82%, 0%)	(125, 55%, 50%) (71%, 0%, 65%, 22%)	(125, 55%, 55%) (62%, 0%, 57%, 20%)
(125, 100%, 50%) (100%, 0%, 92%, 0%)	(125, 50%, 50%) (67%, 0%, 61%, 25%)	(125, 50%, 50%) (67%, 0%, 61%, 25%)
(125, 100%, 45%) (100%, 0%, 92%, 10%)	(125, 45%, 50%) (62%, 0%, 57%, 28%)	(125, 45%, 45%) (62%, 0%, 57%, 35%)
(125, 100%, 40%) (100%, 0%, 92%, 20%)	(125, 40%, 50%) (57%, 0%, 52%, 30%)	(125, 40%, 40%) (57%, 0%, 52%, 44%)
(125, 100%, 35%) (100%, 0%, 92%, 30%)	(125, 35%, 50%) (52%, 0%, 48%, 32%)	(125, 35%, 35%) (52%, 0%, 48%, 53%)
(125, 100%, 30%) (100%, 0%, 92%, 40%)	(125, 30%, 50%) (46%, 0%, 42%, 35%)	(125, 30%, 30%) (46%, 0%, 42%, 61%)
(125, 100%, 25%) (100%, 0%, 92%, 50%)	(125, 25%, 50%) (40%, 0%, 37%, 38%)	(125, 25%, 25%) (40%, 0%, 37%, 69%)
(125, 100%, 20%) (100%, 0%, 92%, 60%)	(125, 20%, 50%) (33%, 0%, 31%, 40%)	(125, 20%, 20%) (33%, 0%, 31%, 76%)
(125, 100%, 15%) (100%, 0%, 92%, 70%)	(125, 15%, 50%) (26%, 0%, 24%, 43%)	(125, 15%, 15%) (26%, 0%, 24%, 83%)
(125, 100%, 10%) (100%, 0%, 92%, 80%)	(125, 10%, 50%) (18%, 0%, 17%, 45%)	(125, 10%, 10%) (18%, 0%, 17%, 89%)
(125, 100%, 5%) (100%, 0%, 92%, 90%)	(125, 5%, 50%) (10%, 0%, 9%, 47%)	(125, 5%, 5%) (10%, 0%, 9%, 95%)
(125, 100%, 0%) (0%, 0%, 0%, 100%)	(125, 0%, 50%) (0%, 0%, 0%, 50%)	(125, 0%, 0%) (0%, 0%, 0%, 100%)

H = 130, S = X%, L = X%	H = 130, S = X%, L = 50%	H = 130, S = 100%, L = X%
(130, 100%, 100%) (0%, 0%, 0%, 0%)	(130, 100%, 50%) (100%, 0%, 83%, 0%)	(130, 100%, 100%) (0%, 0%, 0%, 0%)
(130, 95%, 95%) (10%, 0%, 8%, 0%)	(130, 95%, 50%) (97%, 0%, 81%, 3%)	(130, 100%, 95%) (10%, 0%, 8%, 0%)
(130, 90%, 90%) (18%, 0%, 15%, 1%)	(130, 90%, 50%) (95%, 0%, 79%, 5%)	(130, 100%, 90%) (20%, 0%, 17%, 0%)
(130, 85%, 85%) (26%, 0%, 22%, 2%)	(130, 85%, 50%) (92%, 0%, 77%, 7%)	(130, 100%, 85%) (30%, 0%, 25%, 0%)
(130, 80%, 80%) (33%, 0%, 28%, 4%)	(130, 80%, 50%) (89%, 0%, 74%, 10%)	(130, 100%, 80%) (40%, 0%, 33%, 0%)
(130, 75%, 75%) (40%, 0%, 33%, 6%)	(130, 75%, 50%) (86%, 0%, 71%, 13%)	(130, 100%, 75%) (50%, 0%, 42%, 0%)
(130, 70%, 70%) (46%, 0%, 38%, 9%)	(130, 70%, 50%) (82%, 0%, 69%, 15%)	(130, 100%, 70%) (60%, 0%, 50%, 0%)
(130, 65%, 65%) (52%, 0%, 43%, 12%)	(130, 65%, 50%) (79%, 0%, 66%, 18%)	(130, 100%, 65%) (70%, 0%, 58%, 0%)
(130, 60%, 60%) (57%, 0%, 48%, 16%)	(130, 60%, 50%) (75%, 0%, 63%, 20%)	(130, 100%, 60%) (80%, 0%, 67%, 0%)
(130, 55%, 55%) (62%, 0%, 52%, 20%)	(130, 55%, 50%) (71%, 0%, 59%, 22%)	(130, 100%, 55%) (90%, 0%, 75%, 0%)
(130, 50%, 50%) (67%, 0%, 56%, 25%)	(130, 50%, 50%) (67%, 0%, 56%, 25%)	(130, 100%, 50%) (100%, 0%, 83%, 0%)
(130, 45%, 45%) (62%, 0%, 52%, 35%)	(130, 45%, 50%) (62%, 0%, 52%, 28%)	(130, 100%, 45%) (100%, 0%, 83%, 10%)
(130, 40%, 40%) (57%, 0%, 48%, 44%)	(130, 40%, 50%) (57%, 0%, 48%, 30%)	(130, 100%, 40%) (100%, 0%, 83%, 20%)
(130, 35%, 35%) (52%, 0%, 43%, 53%)	(130, 35%, 50%) (52%, 0%, 43%, 32%)	(130, 100%, 35%) (100%, 0%, 83%, 30%)
(130, 30%, 30%) (46%, 0%, 38%, 61%)	(130, 30%, 50%) (46%, 0%, 38%, 35%)	(130, 100%, 30%) (100%, 0%, 83%, 40%)
(130, 25%, 25%) (40%, 0%, 33%, 69%)	(130, 25%, 50%) (40%, 0%, 33%, 38%)	(130, 100%, 25%) (100%, 0%, 83%, 50%)
(130, 20%, 20%) (33%, 0%, 28%, 76%)	(130, 20%, 50%) (33%, 0%, 28%, 40%)	(130, 100%, 20%) (100%, 0%, 83%, 60%)
(130, 15%, 15%) (26%, 0%, 22%, 83%)	(130, 15%, 50%) (26%, 0%, 22%, 43%)	(130, 100%, 15%) (100%, 0%, 83%, 70%)
(130, 10%, 10%) (18%, 0%, 15%, 89%)	(130, 10%, 50%) (18%, 0%, 15%, 45%)	(130, 100%, 10%) (100%, 0%, 83%, 80%)
(130, 5%, 5%) (10%, 0%, 8%, 95%)	(130, 5%, 50%) (10%, 0%, 8%, 47%)	(130, 100%, 5%) (100%, 0%, 83%, 90%)
(130, 0%, 0%) (0%, 0%, 0%, 100%)	(130, 0%, 50%) (0%, 0%, 0%, 50%)	(130, 100%, 0%) (0%, 0%, 0%, 100%)

H = 135, S = 100%, L = X%	H = 135, S = X%, L = 50%	H = 135, S = X%, L = X%
(135, 100%, 100%) (0%, 0%, 0%, 0%)	(135, 100%, 50%) (100%, 0%, 75%, 0%)	(135, 100%, 100%) (0%, 0%, 0%, 0%)
(135, 100%, 95%) (10%, 0%, 8%, 0%)	(135, 95%, 50%) (97%, 0%, 73%, 3%)	(135, 95%, 95%) (10%, 0%, 7%, 0%)
(135, 100%, 90%) (20%, 0%, 15%, 0%)	(135, 90%, 50%) (95%, 0%, 71%, 5%)	(135, 90%, 90%) (18%, 0%, 14%, 1%)
(135, 100%, 85%) (30%, 0%, 23%, 0%)	(135, 85%, 50%) (92%, 0%, 69%, 7%)	(135, 85%, 85%) (26%, 0%, 20%, 2%)
(135, 100%, 80%) (40%, 0%, 30%, 0%)	(135, 80%, 50%) (89%, 0%, 67%, 10%)	(135, 80%, 80%) (33%, 0%, 25%, 4%)
(135, 100%, 75%) (50%, 0%, 38%, 0%)	(135, 75%, 50%) (86%, 0%, 64%, 13%)	(135, 75%, 75%) (40%, 0%, 30%, 6%)
(135, 100%, 70%) (60%, 0%, 45%, 0%)	(135, 70%, 50%) (82%, 0%, 62%, 15%)	(135, 70%, 70%) (46%, 0%, 35%, 9%)
(135, 100%, 65%) (70%, 0%, 52%, 0%)	(135, 65%, 50%) (79%, 0%, 59%, 18%)	(135, 65%, 65%) (52%, 0%, 39%, 12%)
(135, 100%, 60%) (80%, 0%, 60%, 0%)	(135, 60%, 50%) (75%, 0%, 56%, 20%)	(135, 60%, 60%) (57%, 0%, 43%, 16%)
(135, 100%, 55%) (90%, 0%, 67%, 0%)	(135, 55%, 50%) (71%, 0%, 53%, 22%)	(135, 55%, 55%) (62%, 0%, 47%, 20%)
(135, 100%, 50%) (100%, 0%, 75%, 0%)	(135, 50%, 50%) (67%, 0%, 50%, 25%)	(135, 50%, 50%) (67%, 0%, 50%, 25%)
(135, 100%, 45%) (100%, 0%, 75%, 10%)	(135, 45%, 50%) (62%, 0%, 47%, 28%)	(135, 45%, 45%) (62%, 0%, 47%, 35%)
(135, 100%, 40%) (100%, 0%, 75%, 20%)	(135, 40%, 50%) (57%, 0%, 43%, 30%)	(135, 40%, 40%) (57%, 0%, 43%, 44%)
(135, 100%, 35%) (100%, 0%, 75%, 30%)	(135, 35%, 50%) (52%, 0%, 39%, 32%)	(135, 35%, 35%) (52%, 0%, 39%, 53%)
(135, 100%, 30%) (100%, 0%, 75%, 40%)	(135, 30%, 50%) (46%, 0%, 35%, 35%)	(135, 30%, 30%) (46%, 0%, 35%, 61%)
(135, 100%, 25%) (100%, 0%, 75%, 50%)	(135, 25%, 50%) (40%, 0%, 30%, 38%)	(135, 25%, 25%) (40%, 0%, 30%, 69%)
(135, 100%, 20%) (100%, 0%, 75%, 60%)	(135, 20%, 50%) (33%, 0%, 25%, 40%)	(135, 20%, 20%) (33%, 0%, 25%, 76%)
(135, 100%, 15%) (100%, 0%, 75%, 70%)	(135, 15%, 50%) (26%, 0%, 20%, 43%)	(135, 15%, 15%) (26%, 0%, 20%, 83%)
(135, 100%, 10%) (100%, 0%, 75%, 80%)	(135, 10%, 50%) (18%, 0%, 14%, 45%)	(135, 10%, 10%) (18%, 0%, 14%, 89%)
(135, 100%, 5%) (100%, 0%, 75%, 90%)	(135, 5%, 50%) (10%, 0%, 7%, 47%)	(135, 5%, 5%) (10%, 0%, 7%, 95%)
(135, 100%, 0%) (0%, 0%, 0%, 100%)	(135, 0%, 50%) (0%, 0%, 0%, 50%)	(135, 0%, 0%) (0%, 0%, 0%, 100%)

H = 140, S = X%, L = X%	H = 140, S = X%, L = 50%	H = 140, S = 100%, L = X%
(140, 100%, 100%) (0%, 0%, 0%, 0%)	(140, 100%, 50%) (100%, 0%, 67%, 0%)	(140, 100%, 100%) (0%, 0%, 0%, 0%)
(140, 95%, 95%) (10%, 0%, 6%, 0%)	(140, 95%, 50%) (97%, 0%, 65%, 3%)	(140, 100%, 95%) (10%, 0%, 7%, 0%)
(140, 90%, 90%) (18%, 0%, 12%, 1%)	(140, 90%, 50%) (95%, 0%, 63%, 5%)	(140, 100%, 90%) (20%, 0%, 13%, 0%)
(140, 85%, 85%) (26%, 0%, 17%, 2%)	(140, 85%, 50%) (92%, 0%, 61%, 7%)	(140, 100%, 85%) (30%, 0%, 20%, 0%)
(140, 80%, 80%) (33%, 0%, 22%, 4%)	(140, 80%, 50%) (89%, 0%, 59%, 10%)	(140, 100%, 80%) (40%, 0%, 27%, 0%)
(140, 75%, 75%) (40%, 0%, 27%, 6%)	(140, 75%, 50%) (86%, 0%, 57%, 13%)	(140, 100%, 75%) (50%, 0%, 33%, 0%)
(140, 70%, 70%) (46%, 0%, 31%, 9%)	(140, 70%, 50%) (82%, 0%, 55%, 15%)	(140, 100%, 70%) (60%, 0%, 40%, 0%)
(140, 65%, 65%) (52%, 0%, 35%, 12%)	(140, 65%, 50%) (79%, 0%, 53%, 18%)	(140, 100%, 65%) (70%, 0%, 47%, 0%)
(140, 60%, 60%) (57%, 0%, 38%, 16%)	(140, 60%, 50%) (75%, 0%, 50%, 20%)	(140, 100%, 60%) (80%, 0%, 53%, 0%)
(140, 55%, 55%) (62%, 0%, 41%, 20%)	(140, 55%, 50%) (71%, 0%, 47%, 22%)	(140, 100%, 55%) (90%, 0%, 60%, 0%)
(140, 50%, 50%) (67%, 0%, 44%, 25%)	(140, 50%, 50%) (67%, 0%, 44%, 25%)	(140, 100%, 50%) (100%, 0%, 67%, 0%)
(140, 45%, 45%) (62%, 0%, 41%, 35%)	(140, 45%, 50%) (62%, 0%, 41%, 28%)	(140, 100%, 45%) (100%, 0%, 67%, 10%)
(140, 40%, 40%) (57%, 0%, 38%, 44%)	(140, 40%, 50%) (57%, 0%, 38%, 30%)	(140, 100%, 40%) (100%, 0%, 67%, 20%)
(140, 35%, 35%) (52%, 0%, 35%, 53%)	(140, 35%, 50%) (52%, 0%, 35%, 32%)	(140, 100%, 35%) (100%, 0%, 67%, 30%)
(140, 30%, 30%) (46%, 0%, 31%, 61%)	(140, 30%, 50%) (46%, 0%, 31%, 35%)	(140, 100%, 30%) (100%, 0%, 67%, 40%)
(140, 25%, 25%) (40%, 0%, 27%, 69%)	(140, 25%, 50%) (40%, 0%, 27%, 38%)	(140, 100%, 25%) (100%, 0%, 67%, 50%)
(140, 20%, 20%) (33%, 0%, 22%, 76%)	(140, 20%, 50%) (33%, 0%, 22%, 40%)	(140, 100%, 20%) (100%, 0%, 67%, 60%)
(140, 15%, 15%) (26%, 0%, 17%, 83%)	(140, 15%, 50%) (26%, 0%, 17%, 43%)	(140, 100%, 15%) (100%, 0%, 67%, 70%)
(140, 10%, 10%) (18%, 0%, 12%, 89%)	(140, 10%, 50%) (18%, 0%, 12%, 45%)	(140, 100%, 10%) (100%, 0%, 67%, 80%)
(140, 5%, 5%) (10%, 0%, 6%, 95%)	(140, 5%, 50%) (10%, 0%, 6%, 47%)	(140, 100%, 5%) (100%, 0%, 67%, 90%)
(140, 0%, 0%) (0%, 0%, 0%, 100%)	(140, 0%, 50%) (0%, 0%, 0%, 50%)	(140, 100%, 0%) (0%, 0%, 0%, 100%)

H = 145, S = 100%, L = X%	H = 145, S = X%, L = 50%	H = 145, S = X%, L = X%
(145, 100%, 100%) (0%, 0%, 0%, 0%)	(145, 100%, 50%) (100%, 0%, 58%, 0%)	(145, 100%, 100%) (0%, 0%, 0%, 0%)
(145, 100%, 95%) (10%, 0%, 6%, 0%)	(145, 95%, 50%) (97%, 0%, 57%, 3%)	(145, 95%, 95%) (10%, 0%, 6%, 0%)
(145, 100%, 90%) (20%, 0%, 12%, 0%)	(145, 90%, 50%) (95%, 0%, 55%, 5%)	(145, 90%, 90%) (18%, 0%, 11%, 1%)
(145, 100%, 85%) (30%, 0%, 18%, 0%)	(145, 85%, 50%) (92%, 0%, 54%, 7%)	(145, 85%, 85%) (26%, 0%, 15%, 2%)
(145, 100%, 80%) (40%, 0%, 23%, 0%)	(145, 80%, 50%) (89%, 0%, 52%, 10%)	(145, 80%, 80%) (33%, 0%, 19%, 4%)
(145, 100%, 75%) (50%, 0%, 29%, 0%)	(145, 75%, 50%) (86%, 0%, 50%, 13%)	(145, 75%, 75%) (40%, 0%, 23%, 6%)
(145, 100%, 70%) (60%, 0%, 35%, 0%)	(145, 70%, 50%) (82%, 0%, 48%, 15%)	(145, 70%, 70%) (46%, 0%, 27%, 9%)
(145, 100%, 65%) (70%, 0%, 41%, 0%)	(145, 65%, 50%) (79%, 0%, 46%, 18%)	(145, 65%, 65%) (52%, 0%, 30%, 12%)
(145, 100%, 60%) (80%, 0%, 47%, 0%)	(145, 60%, 50%) (75%, 0%, 44%, 20%)	(145, 60%, 60%) (57%, 0%, 33%, 16%)
(145, 100%, 55%) (90%, 0%, 53%, 0%)	(145, 55%, 50%) (71%, 0%, 41%, 22%)	(145, 55%, 55%) (62%, 0%, 36%, 20%)
(145, 100%, 50%) (100%, 0%, 58%, 0%)	(145, 50%, 50%) (67%, 0%, 39%, 25%)	(145, 50%, 50%) (67%, 0%, 39%, 25%)
(145, 100%, 45%) (100%, 0%, 58%, 10%)	(145, 45%, 50%) (62%, 0%, 36%, 28%)	(145, 45%, 45%) (62%, 0%, 36%, 35%)
(145, 100%, 40%) (100%, 0%, 58%, 20%)	(145, 40%, 50%) (57%, 0%, 33%, 30%)	(145, 40%, 40%) (57%, 0%, 33%, 44%)
(145, 100%, 35%) (100%, 0%, 58%, 30%)	(145, 35%, 50%) (52%, 0%, 30%, 32%)	(145, 35%, 35%) (52%, 0%, 30%, 53%)
(145, 100%, 30%) (100%, 0%, 58%, 40%)	(145, 30%, 50%) (46%, 0%, 27%, 35%)	(145, 30%, 30%) (46%, 0%, 27%, 61%)
(145, 100%, 25%) (100%, 0%, 58%, 50%)	(145, 25%, 50%) (40%, 0%, 23%, 38%)	(145, 25%, 25%) (40%, 0%, 23%, 69%)
(145, 100%, 20%) (100%, 0%, 58%, 60%)	(145, 20%, 50%) (33%, 0%, 19%, 40%)	(145, 20%, 20%) (33%, 0%, 19%, 76%)
(145, 100%, 15%) (100%, 0%, 58%, 70%)	(145, 15%, 50%) (26%, 0%, 15%, 43%)	(145, 15%, 15%) (26%, 0%, 15%, 83%)
(145, 100%, 10%) (100%, 0%, 58%, 80%)	(145, 10%, 50%) (18%, 0%, 11%, 45%)	(145, 10%, 10%) (18%, 0%, 11%, 89%)
(145, 100%, 5%) (100%, 0%, 58%, 90%)	(145, 5%, 50%) (10%, 0%, 6%, 47%)	(145, 5%, 5%) (10%, 0%, 6%, 95%)
(145, 100%, 0%) (0%, 0%, 0%, 100%)	(145, 0%, 50%) (0%, 0%, 0%, 50%)	(145, 0%, 0%) (0%, 0%, 0%, 100%)

H = 150, S = X%, L = X%	H = 150, S = X%, L = 50%	H = 150, S = 100%, L = X%
(150, 100%, 100%) (0%, 0%, 0%, 0%)	(150, 100%, 50%) (100%, 0%, 50%, 0%)	(150, 100%, 100%) (0%, 0%, 0%, 0%)
(150, 95%, 95%) (10%, 0%, 5%, 0%)	(150, 95%, 50%) (97%, 0%, 49%, 3%)	(150, 100%, 95%) (10%, 0%, 5%, 0%)
(150, 90%, 90%) (18%, 0%, 9%, 1%)	(150, 90%, 50%) (95%, 0%, 47%, 5%)	(150, 100%, 90%) (20%, 0%, 10%, 0%)
(150, 85%, 85%) (26%, 0%, 13%, 2%)	(150, 85%, 50%) (92%, 0%, 46%, 7%)	(150, 100%, 85%) (30%, 0%, 15%, 0%)
(150, 80%, 80%) (33%, 0%, 17%, 4%)	(150, 80%, 50%) (89%, 0%, 44%, 10%)	(150, 100%, 80%) (40%, 0%, 20%, 0%)
(150, 75%, 75%) (40%, 0%, 20%, 6%)	(150, 75%, 50%) (86%, 0%, 43%, 13%)	(150, 100%, 75%) (50%, 0%, 25%, 0%)
(150, 70%, 70%) (46%, 0%, 23%, 9%)	(150, 70%, 50%) (82%, 0%, 41%, 15%)	(150, 100%, 70%) (60%, 0%, 30%, 0%)
(150, 65%, 65%) (52%, 0%, 26%, 12%)	(150, 65%, 50%) (79%, 0%, 49%, 18%)	(150, 100%, 65%) (70%, 0%, 35%, 0%)
(150, 60%, 60%) (57%, 0%, 29%, 16%)	(150, 60%, 50%) (75%, 0%, 38%, 20%)	(150, 100%, 60%) (80%, 0%, 40%, 0%)
(150, 55%, 55%) (62%, 0%, 31%, 20%)	(150, 55%, 50%) (71%, 0%, 35%, 22%)	(150, 100%, 55%) (90%, 0%, 45%, 0%)
(150, 50%, 50%) (67%, 0%, 33%, 25%)	(150, 50%, 50%) (67%, 0%, 33%, 25%)	(150, 100%, 50%) (100%, 0%, 50%, 0%)
(150, 45%, 45%) (62%, 0%, 31%, 35%)	(150, 45%, 50%) (62%, 0%, 31%, 28%)	(150, 100%, 45%) (100%, 0%, 50%, 10%)
(150, 40%, 40%) (57%, 0%, 29%, 44%)	(150, 40%, 50%) (57%, 0%, 29%, 30%)	(150, 100%, 40%) (100%, 0%, 50%, 20%)
(150, 35%, 35%) (52%, 0%, 26%, 53%)	(150, 35%, 50%) (52%, 0%, 26%, 32%)	(150, 100%, 35%) (100%, 0%, 50%, 30%)
(150, 30%, 30%) (46%, 0%, 23%, 61%)	(150, 30%, 50%) (46%, 0%, 23%, 35%)	(150, 100%, 30%) (100%, 0%, 50%, 40%)
(150, 25%, 25%) (40%, 0%, 20%, 69%)	(150, 25%, 50%) (40%, 0%, 20%, 38%)	(150, 100%, 25%) (100%, 0%, 50%, 50%)
(150, 20%, 20%) (33%, 0%, 17%, 76%)	(150, 20%, 50%) (33%, 0%, 17%, 40%)	(150, 100%, 20%) (100%, 0%, 50%, 60%)
(150, 15%, 15%) (26%, 0%, 13%, 83%)	(150, 15%, 50%) (26%, 0%, 13%, 43%)	(150, 100%, 15%) (100%, 0%, 50%, 70%)
(150, 10%, 10%) (18%, 0%, 9%, 89%)	(150, 10%, 50%) (18%, 0%, 9%, 45%)	(150, 100%, 10%) (100%, 0%, 50%, 80%)
(150, 5%, 5%) (10%, 0%, 5%, 95%)	(150, 5%, 50%) (10%, 0%, 5%, 47%)	(150, 100%, 5%) (100%, 0%, 50%, 90%)
(150, 0%, 0%) (0%, 0%, 0%, 100%)	(150, 0%, 50%) (0%, 0%, 0%, 50%)	(150, 100%, 0%) (0%, 0%, 0%, 100%)

H = 155, S = 100%, L = X%	H = 155, S = X%, L = 50%	H = 155, S = X%, L = X%
(155, 100%, 100%) (0%, 0%, 0%, 0%)	(155, 100%, 50%) (100%, 0%, 42%, 0%)	(155, 100%, 100%) (0%, 0%, 0%, 0%)
(155, 100%, 95%) (10%, 0%, 4%, 0%)	(155, 95%, 50%) (97%, 0%, 41%, 3%)	(155, 95%, 95%) (10%, 0%, 4%, 0%)
(155, 100%, 90%) (20%, 0%, 8%, 0%)	(155, 90%, 50%) (95%, 0%, 39%, 5%)	(155, 90%, 90%) (18%, 0%, 8%, 1%)
(155, 100%, 85%) (30%, 0%, 13%, 0%)	(155, 85%, 50%) (92%, 0%, 38%, 7%)	(155, 85%, 85%) (26%, 0%, 11%, 2%)
(155, 100%, 80%) (40%, 0%, 17%, 0%)	(155, 80%, 50%) (89%, 0%, 37%, 10%)	(155, 80%, 80%) (33%, 0%, 14%, 4%)
(155, 100%, 75%) (50%, 0%, 21%, 0%)	(155, 75%, 50%) (86%, 0%, 36%, 13%)	(155, 75%, 75%) (40%, 0%, 17%, 6%)
(155, 100%, 70%) (60%, 0%, 25%, 0%)	(155, 70%, 50%) (82%, 0%, 34%, 15%)	(155, 70%, 70%) (46%, 0%, 19%, 9%)
(155, 100%, 65%) (70%, 0%, 29%, 0%)	(155, 65%, 50%) (79%, 0%, 33%, 18%)	(155, 65%, 65%) (52%, 0%, 22%, 12%)
(155, 100%, 60%) (80%, 0%, 33%, 0%)	(155, 60%, 50%) (75%, 0%, 31%, 20%)	(155, 60%, 60%) (57%, 0%, 24%, 16%)
(155, 100%, 55%) (90%, 0%, 37%, 0%)	(155, 55%, 50%) (71%, 0%, 30%, 22%)	(155, 55%, 55%) (62%, 0%, 26%, 20%)
(155, 100%, 50%) (100%, 0%, 42%, 0%)	(155, 50%, 50%) (67%, 0%, 28%, 25%)	(155, 50%, 50%) (67%, 0%, 28%, 25%)
(155, 100%, 45%) (100%, 0%, 42%, 10%)	(155, 45%, 50%) (62%, 0%, 26%, 28%)	(155, 45%, 45%) (62%, 0%, 26%, 35%)
(155, 100%, 40%) (100%, 0%, 42%, 20%)	(155, 40%, 50%) (57%, 0%, 24%, 30%)	(155, 40%, 40%) (57%, 0%, 24%, 44%)
(155, 100%, 35%) (100%, 0%, 42%, 30%)	(155, 35%, 50%) (52%, 0%, 22%, 32%)	(155, 35%, 35%) (52%, 0%, 22%, 53%)
(155, 100%, 30%) (100%, 0%, 42%, 40%)	(155, 30%, 50%) (46%, 0%, 19%, 35%)	(155, 30%, 30%) (46%, 0%, 19%, 61%)
(155, 100%, 25%) (100%, 0%, 42%, 50%)	(155, 25%, 50%) (40%, 0%, 17%, 38%)	(155, 25%, 25%) (40%, 0%, 17%, 69%)
(155, 100%, 20%) (100%, 0%, 42%, 60%)	(155, 20%, 50%) (33%, 0%, 14%, 40%)	(155, 20%, 20%) (33%, 0%, 14%, 76%)
(155, 100%, 15%) (100%, 0%, 42%, 70%)	(155, 15%, 50%) (26%, 0%, 11%, 43%)	(155, 15%, 15%) (26%, 0%, 11%, 83%)
(155, 100%, 10%) (100%, 0%, 42%, 80%)	(155, 10%, 50%) (18%, 0%, 8%, 45%)	(155, 10%, 10%) (18%, 0%, 8%, 89%)
(155, 100%, 5%) (100%, 0%, 42%, 90%)	(155, 5%, 50%) (10%, 0%, 4%, 47%)	(155, 5%, 5%) (10%, 0%, 4%, 95%)
(155, 100%, 0%) (0%, 0%, 0%, 100%)	(155, 0%, 50%) (0%, 0%, 0%, 50%)	(155, 0%, 0%) (0%, 0%, 0%, 100%)

H = 160, S = X%, L = X%	H = 160, S = X%, L = 50%	H = 160, S = 100%, L = X%
(160, 100%, 100%) (0%, 0%, 0%, 0%)	(160, 100%, 50%) (100%, 0%, 33%, 0%)	(160, 100%, 100%) (0%, 0%, 0%, 0%)
(160, 95%, 95%) (10%, 0%, 3%, 0%)	(160, 95%, 50%) (97%, 0%, 32%, 3%)	(160, 100%, 95%) (10%, 0%, 3%, 0%)
(160, 90%, 90%) (18%, 0%, 6%, 1%)	(160, 90%, 50%) (95%, 0%, 32%, 5%)	(160, 100%, 90%) (20%, 0%, 7%, 0%)
(160, 85%, 85%) (26%, 0%, 9%, 2%)	(160, 85%, 50%) (92%, 0%, 31%, 7%)	(160, 100%, 85%) (30%, 0%, 10%, 0%)
(160, 80%, 80%) (33%, 0%, 11%, 4%)	(160, 80%, 50%) (89%, 0%, 30%, 10%)	(160, 100%, 80%) (40%, 0%, 13%, 0%)
(160, 75%, 75%) (40%, 0%, 13%, 6%)	(160, 75%, 50%) (86%, 0%, 29%, 13%)	(160, 100%, 75%) (50%, 0%, 17%, 0%)
(160, 70%, 70%) (46%, 0%, 15%, 9%)	(160, 70%, 50%) (82%, 0%, 27%, 15%)	(160, 100%, 70%) (60%, 0%, 20%, 0%)
(160, 65%, 65%) (52%, 0%, 17%, 12%)	(160, 65%, 50%) (79%, 0%, 26%, 18%)	(160, 100%, 65%) (70%, 0%, 23%, 0%)
(160, 60%, 60%) (57%, 0%, 19%, 16%)	(160, 60%, 50%) (75%, 0%, 25%, 20%)	(160, 100%, 60%) (80%, 0%, 27%, 0%)
(160, 55%, 55%) (62%, 0%, 21%, 20%)	(160, 55%, 50%) (71%, 0%, 24%, 22%)	(160, 100%, 55%) (90%, 0%, 30%, 0%)
(160, 50%, 50%) (67%, 0%, 22%, 25%)	(160, 50%, 50%) (67%, 0%, 22%, 25%)	(160, 100%, 50%) (100%, 0%, 33%, 0%)
(160, 45%, 45%) (62%, 0%, 21%, 35%)	(160, 45%, 50%) (62%, 0%, 21%, 28%)	(160, 100%, 45%) (100%, 0%, 33%, 10%)
(160, 40%, 40%) (57%, 0%, 19%, 44%)	(160, 40%, 50%) (57%, 0%, 19%, 30%)	(160, 100%, 40%) (100%, 0%, 33%, 20%)
(160, 35%, 35%) (52%, 0%, 17%, 53%)	(160, 35%, 50%) (52%, 0%, 17%, 32%)	(160, 100%, 35%) (100%, 0%, 33%, 30%)
(160, 30%, 30%) (46%, 0%, 15%, 61%)	(160, 30%, 50%) (46%, 0%, 15%, 35%)	(160, 100%, 30%) (100%, 0%, 33%, 40%)
(160, 25%, 25%) (40%, 0%, 13%, 69%)	(160, 25%, 50%) (40%, 0%, 13%, 38%)	(160, 100%, 25%) (100%, 0%, 33%, 50%)
(160, 20%, 20%) (33%, 0%, 11%, 76%)	(160, 20%, 50%) (33%, 0%, 11%, 40%)	(160, 100%, 20%) (100%, 0%, 33%, 60%)
(160, 15%, 15%) (26%, 0%, 9%, 83%)	(160, 15%, 50%) (26%, 0%, 9%, 43%)	(160, 100%, 15%) (100%, 0%, 33%, 70%)
(160, 10%, 10%) (18%, 0%, 6%, 89%)	(160, 10%, 50%) (18%, 0%, 6%, 45%)	(160, 100%, 10%) (100%, 0%, 33%, 80%)
(160, 5%, 5%) (10%, 0%, 3%, 95%)	(160, 5%, 50%) (10%, 0%, 3%, 47%)	(160, 100%, 5%) (100%, 0%, 33%, 90%)
(160, 0%, 0%) (0%, 0%, 0%, 100%)	(160, 0%, 50%) (0%, 0%, 0%, 50%)	(160, 100%, 0%) (0%, 0%, 0%, 100%)

H = 165, S = 100%, L = X%	H = 165, S = X%, L = 50%	H = 165, S = X%, L = X%
(165, 100%, 100%) (0%, 0%, 0%, 0%)	(165, 100%, 50%) (100%, 0%, 25%, 0%)	(165, 100%, 100%) (0%, 0%, 0%, 0%)
(165, 100%, 95%) (10%, 0%, 3%, 0%)	(165, 95%, 50%) (97%, 0%, 24%, 3%)	(165, 95%, 95%) (10%, 0%, 2%, 0%)
(165, 100%, 90%) (20%, 0%, 5%, 0%)	(165, 90%, 50%) (95%, 0%, 24%, 5%)	(165, 90%, 90%) (18%, 0%, 5%, 1%)
(165, 100%, 85%) (30%, 0%, 7%, 0%)	(165, 85%, 50%) (92%, 0%, 23%, 7%)	(165, 85%, 85%) (26%, 0%, 7%, 2%)
(165, 100%, 80%) (40%, 0%, 10%, 0%)	(165, 80%, 50%) (89%, 0%, 22%, 10%)	(165, 80%, 80%) (33%, 0%, 8%, 4%)
(165, 100%, 75%) (50%, 0%, 13%, 0%)	(165, 75%, 50%) (86%, 0%, 21%, 13%)	(165, 75%, 75%) (40%, 0%, 10%, 6%)
(165, 100%, 70%) (60%, 0%, 15%, 0%)	(165, 70%, 50%) (82%, 0%, 21%, 15%)	(165, 70%, 70%) (46%, 0%, 12%, 9%)
(165, 100%, 65%) (70%, 0%, 17%, 0%)	(165, 65%, 50%) (79%, 0%, 20%, 18%)	(165, 65%, 65%) (52%, 0%, 13%, 12%)
(165, 100%, 60%) (80%, 0%, 20%, 0%)	(165, 60%, 50%) (75%, 0%, 19%, 20%)	(165, 60%, 60%) (57%, 0%, 14%, 16%)
(165, 100%, 55%) (90%, 0%, 22%, 0%)	(165, 55%, 50%) (71%, 0%, 18%, 22%)	(165, 55%, 55%) (62%, 0%, 16%, 20%)
(165, 100%, 50%) (100%, 0%, 25%, 0%)	(165, 50%, 50%) (67%, 0%, 17%, 25%)	(165, 50%, 50%) (67%, 0%, 17%, 25%)
(165, 100%, 45%) (100%, 0%, 25%, 10%)	(165, 45%, 50%) (62%, 0%, 16%, 28%)	(165, 45%, 45%) (62%, 0%, 16%, 35%)
(165, 100%, 40%) (100%, 0%, 25%, 20%)	(165, 40%, 50%) (57%, 0%, 14%, 30%)	(165, 40%, 40%) (57%, 0%, 14%, 44%)
(165, 100%, 35%) (100%, 0%, 25%, 30%)	(165, 35%, 50%) (52%, 0%, 13%, 32%)	(165, 35%, 35%) (52%, 0%, 13%, 53%)
(165, 100%, 30%) (100%, 0%, 25%, 40%)	(165, 30%, 50%) (46%, 0%, 12%, 35%)	(165, 30%, 30%) (46%, 0%, 12%, 61%)
(165, 100%, 25%) (100%, 0%, 25%, 50%)	(165, 25%, 50%) (40%, 0%, 10%, 38%)	(165, 25%, 25%) (40%, 0%, 10%, 69%)
(165, 100%, 20%) (100%, 0%, 25%, 60%)	(165, 20%, 50%) (33%, 0%, 8%, 40%)	(165, 20%, 20%) (33%, 0%, 8%, 76%)
(165, 100%, 15%) (100%, 0%, 25%, 70%)	(165, 15%, 50%) (26%, 0%, 7%, 43%)	(165, 15%, 15%) (26%, 0%, 7%, 83%)
(165, 100%, 10%) (100%, 0%, 25%, 80%)	(165, 10%, 50%) (18%, 0%, 5%, 45%)	(165, 10%, 10%) (18%, 0%, 5%, 89%)
(165, 100%, 5%) (100%, 0%, 25%, 90%)	(165, 5%, 50%) (10%, 0%, 2%, 47%)	(165, 5%, 5%) (10%, 0%, 2%, 95%)
(165, 100%, 0%) (0%, 0%, 0%, 100%)	(165, 0%, 50%) (0%, 0%, 0%, 50%)	(165, 0%, 0%) (0%, 0%, 0%, 100%)

H = 170, S = X%, L = X%	H = 170, S = X%, L = 50%	H = 170, S = 100%, L = X%
(170, 100%, 100%) (0%, 0%, 0%, 0%)	(170, 100%, 50%) (100%, 0%, 17%, 0%)	(170, 100%, 100%) (0%, 0%, 0%, 0%)
(170, 95%, 95%) (10%, 0%, 2%, 0%)	(170, 95%, 50%) (97%, 0%, 16%, 3%)	(170, 100%, 95%) (10%, 0%, 2%, 0%)
(170, 90%, 90%) (18%, 0%, 3%, 1%)	(170, 90%, 50%) (95%, 0%, 16%, 5%)	(170, 100%, 90%) (20%, 0%, 3%, 0%)
(170, 85%, 85%) (26%, 0%, 4%, 2%)	(170, 85%, 50%) (92%, 0%, 15%, 7%)	(170, 100%, 85%) (30%, 0%, 5%, 0%)
(170, 80%, 80%) (33%, 0%, 6%, 4%)	(170, 80%, 50%) (89%, 0%, 15%, 10%)	(170, 100%, 80%) (40%, 0%, 7%, 0%)
(170, 75%, 75%) (40%, 0%, 7%, 6%)	(170, 75%, 50%) (86%, 0%, 14%, 13%)	(170, 100%, 75%) (50%, 0%, 8%, 0%)
(170, 70%, 70%) (46%, 0%, 8%, 9%)	(170, 70%, 50%) (82%, 0%, 14%, 15%)	(170, 100%, 70%) (60%, 0%, 10%, 0%)
(170, 65%, 65%) (52%, 0%, 9%, 12%)	(170, 65%, 50%) (79%, 0%, 13%, 18%)	(170, 100%, 65%) (70%, 0%, 12%, 0%)
(170, 60%, 60%) (57%, 0%, 10%, 16%)	(170, 60%, 50%) (75%, 0%, 12%, 20%)	(170, 100%, 60%) (80%, 0%, 13%, 0%)
(170, 55%, 55%) (62%, 0%, 10%, 20%)	(170, 55%, 50%) (71%, 0%, 12%, 22%)	(170, 100%, 55%) (90%, 0%, 15%, 0%)
(170, 50%, 50%) (67%, 0%, 11%, 25%)	(170, 50%, 50%) (67%, 0%, 11%, 25%)	(170, 100%, 50%) (100%, 0%, 17%, 0%)
(170, 45%, 45%) (62%, 0%, 10%, 35%)	(170, 45%, 50%) (62%, 0%, 10%, 28%)	(170, 100%, 45%) (100%, 0%, 17%, 10%)
(170, 40%, 40%) (57%, 0%, 10%, 44%)	(170, 40%, 50%) (57%, 0%, 10%, 30%)	(170, 100%, 40%) (100%, 0%, 17%, 20%)
(170, 35%, 35%) (52%, 0%, 9%, 53%)	(170, 35%, 50%) (52%, 0%, 9%, 32%)	(170, 100%, 35%) (100%, 0%, 17%, 30%)
(170, 30%, 30%) (46%, 0%, 8%, 61%)	(170, 30%, 50%) (46%, 0%, 8%, 35%)	(170, 100%, 30%) (100%, 0%, 17%, 40%)
(170, 25%, 25%) (40%, 0%, 7%, 69%)	(170, 25%, 50%) (40%, 0%, 7%, 38%)	(170, 100%, 25%) (100%, 0%, 17%, 50%)
(170, 20%, 20%) (33%, 0%, 6%, 76%)	(170, 20%, 50%) (33%, 0%, 6%, 40%)	(170, 100%, 20%) (100%, 0%, 17%, 60%)
(170, 15%, 15%) (26%, 0%, 4%, 83%)	(170, 15%, 50%) (26%, 0%, 4%, 43%)	(170, 100%, 15%) (100%, 0%, 17%, 70%)
(170, 10%, 10%) (18%, 0%, 3%, 89%)	(170, 10%, 50%) (18%, 0%, 3%, 45%)	(170, 100%, 10%) (100%, 0%, 17%, 80%)
(170, 5%, 5%) (10%, 0%, 2%, 95%)	(170, 5%, 50%) (10%, 0%, 2%, 47%)	(170, 100%, 5%) (100%, 0%, 17%, 90%)
(170, 0%, 0%) (0%, 0%, 0%, 100%)	(170, 0%, 50%) (0%, 0%, 0%, 50%)	(170, 100%, 0%) (0%, 0%, 0%, 100%)

H = 175, S = 100%, L = X%	H = 175, S = X%, L = 50%	H = 175, S = X%, L = X%
(175, 100%, 100%) (0%, 0%, 0%, 0%)	(175, 100%, 50%) (100%, 0%, 8%, 0%)	(175, 100%, 100%) (0%, 0%, 0%, 0%)
(175, 100%, 95%) (10%, 0%, 1%, 0%)	(175, 95%, 50%) (97%, 0%, 8%, 3%)	(175, 95%, 95%) (10%, 0%, 1%, 0%)
(175, 100%, 90%) (20%, 0%, 2%, 0%)	(175, 90%, 50%) (95%, 0%, 8%, 5%)	(175, 90%, 90%) (18%, 0%, 2%, 1%)
(175, 100%, 85%) (30%, 0%, 3%, 0%)	(175, 85%, 50%) (92%, 0%, 8%, 7%)	(175, 85%, 85%) (26%, 0%, 2%, 2%)
(175, 100%, 80%) (40%, 0%, 3%, 0%)	(175, 80%, 50%) (89%, 0%, 7%, 10%)	(175, 80%, 80%) (33%, 0%, 3%, 4%)
(175, 100%, 75%) (50%, 0%, 4%, 0%)	(175, 75%, 50%) (86%, 0%, 7%, 13%)	(175, 75%, 75%) (40%, 0%, 3%, 6%)
(175, 100%, 70%) (60%, 0%, 5%, 0%)	(175, 70%, 50%) (82%, 0%, 7%, 15%)	(175, 70%, 70%) (46%, 0%, 4%, 9%)
(175, 100%, 65%) (70%, 0%, 6%, 0%)	(175, 65%, 50%) (79%, 0%, 7%, 18%)	(175, 65%, 65%) (52%, 0%, 4%, 12%)
(175, 100%, 60%) (80%, 0%, 7%, 0%)	(175, 60%, 50%) (75%, 0%, 6%, 20%)	(175, 60%, 60%) (57%, 0%, 5%, 16%)
(175, 100%, 55%) (90%, 0%, 8%, 0%)	(175, 55%, 50%) (71%, 0%, 6%, 22%)	(175, 55%, 55%) (62%, 0%, 5%, 20%)
(175, 100%, 50%) (100%, 0%, 8%, 0%)	(175, 50%, 50%) (67%, 0%, 6%, 25%)	(175, 50%, 50%) (67%, 0%, 6%, 25%)
(175, 100%, 45%) (100%, 0%, 8%, 10%)	(175, 45%, 50%) (62%, 0%, 5%, 28%)	(175, 45%, 45%) (62%, 0%, 5%, 35%)
(175, 100%, 40%) (100%, 0%, 8%, 20%)	(175, 40%, 50%) (57%, 0%, 5%, 30%)	(175, 40%, 40%) (57%, 0%, 5%, 44%)
(175, 100%, 35%) (100%, 0%, 8%, 30%)	(175, 35%, 50%) (52%, 0%, 4%, 32%)	(175, 35%, 35%) (52%, 0%, 4%, 53%)
(175, 100%, 30%) (100%, 0%, 8%, 40%)	(175, 30%, 50%) (46%, 0%, 4%, 35%)	(175, 30%, 30%) (46%, 0%, 4%, 61%)
(175, 100%, 25%) (100%, 0%, 8%, 50%)	(175, 25%, 50%) (40%, 0%, 3%, 38%)	(175, 25%, 25%) (40%, 0%, 3%, 69%)
(175, 100%, 20%) (100%, 0%, 8%, 60%)	(175, 20%, 50%) (33%, 0%, 3%, 40%)	(175, 20%, 20%) (33%, 0%, 3%, 76%)
(175, 100%, 15%) (100%, 0%, 8%, 70%)	(175, 15%, 50%) (26%, 0%, 2%, 43%)	(175, 15%, 15%) (26%, 0%, 2%, 83%)
(175, 100%, 10%) (100%, 0%, 8%, 80%)	(175, 10%, 50%) (18%, 0%, 2%, 45%)	(175, 10%, 10%) (18%, 0%, 2%, 89%)
(175, 100%, 5%) (100%, 0%, 8%, 90%)	(175, 5%, 50%) (10%, 0%, 1%, 47%)	(175, 5%, 5%) (10%, 0%, 1%, 95%)
(175, 100%, 0%) (0%, 0%, 0%, 100%)	(175, 0%, 50%) (0%, 0%, 0%, 50%)	(175, 0%, 0%) (0%, 0%, 0%, 100%)

H = 180, S = X%, L = X%	H = 180, S = X%, L = 50%	H = 180, S = 100%, L = X%
(180, 100%, 100%) (0%, 0%, 0%, 0%)	(180, 100%, 50%) (100%, 0%, 0%, 0%)	(180, 100%, 100%) (0%, 0%, 0%, 0%)
(180, 95%, 95%) (10%, 0%, 0%, 0%)	(180, 95%, 50%) (97%, 0%, 0%, 3%)	(180, 100%, 95%) (10%, 0%, 0%, 0%)
(180, 90%, 90%) (18%, 0%, 0%, 1%)	(180, 90%, 50%) (95%, 0%, 0%, 5%)	(180, 100%, 90%) (20%, 0%, 0%, 0%)
(180, 85%, 85%) (26%, 0%, 0%, 2%)	(180, 85%, 50%) (92%, 0%, 0%, 7%)	(180, 100%, 85%) (30%, 0%, 0%, 0%)
(180, 80%, 80%) (33%, 0%, 0%, 4%)	(180, 80%, 50%) (89%, 0%, 0%, 10%)	(180, 100%, 80%) (40%, 0%, 0%, 0%)
(180, 75%, 75%) (40%, 0%, 0%, 6%)	(180, 75%, 50%) (86%, 0%, 0%, 13%)	(180, 100%, 75%) (50%, 0%, 0%, 0%)
(180, 70%, 70%) (46%, 0%, 0%, 9%)	(180, 70%, 50%) (82%, 0%, 0%, 15%)	(180, 100%, 70%) (60%, 0%, 0%, 0%)
(180, 65%, 65%) (52%, 0%, 0%, 12%)	(180, 65%, 50%) (79%, 0%, 0%, 18%)	(180, 100%, 65%) (70%, 0%, 0%, 0%)
(180, 60%, 60%) (57%, 0%, 0%, 16%)	(180, 60%, 50%) (75%, 0%, 0%, 20%)	(180, 100%, 60%) (80%, 0%, 0%, 0%)
(180, 55%, 55%) (62%, 0%, 0%, 20%)	(180, 55%, 50%) (71%, 0%, 0%, 22%)	(180, 100%, 55%) (90%, 0%, 0%, 0%)
(180, 50%, 50%) (67%, 0%, 0%, 25%)	(180, 50%, 50%) (67%, 0%, 0%, 25%)	(180, 100%, 50%) (100%, 0%, 0%, 0%)
(180, 45%, 45%) (62%, 0%, 0%, 35%)	(180, 45%, 50%) (62%, 0%, 0%, 28%)	(180, 100%, 45%) (100%, 0%, 0%, 10%)
(180, 40, 40%) (57%, 0%, 0%, 44%)	(180, 40%, 50%) (57%, 0%, 0%, 30%)	(180, 100%, 40%) (100%, 0%, 0%, 20%)
(180, 35%, 35%) (52%, 0%, 0%, 53%)	(180, 35%, 50%) (52%, 0%, 0%, 32%)	(180, 100%, 35%) (100%, 0%, 0%, 30%)
(180, 30%, 30%) (46%, 0%, 0%, 61%)	(180, 30%, 50%) (46%, 0%, 0%, 35%)	(180, 100%, 30%) (100%, 0%, 0%, 40%)
(180, 25%, 25%) (40%, 0%, 0%, 69%)	(180, 25%, 50%) (40%, 0%, 0%, 38%)	(180, 100%, 25%) (100%, 0%, 0%, 50%)
(180, 20%, 20%) (33%, 0%, 0%, 76%)	(180, 20%, 50%) (33%, 0%, 0%, 40%)	(180, 100%, 20%) (100%, 0%, 0%, 60%)
(180, 15%, 15%) (26%, 0%, 0%, 83%)	(180, 15%, 50%) (26%, 0%, 0%, 43%)	(180, 100%, 15%) (100%, 0%, 0%, 70%)
(180, 10%, 10%) (18%, 0%, 0%, 89%)	(180, 10%, 50%) (18%, 0%, 0%, 45%)	(180, 100%, 10%) (100%, 0%, 0%, 80%)
(180, 5%, 5%) (10%, 0%, 0%, 95%)	(180, 5%, 50%) (10%, 0%, 0%, 47%)	(180, 100%, 5%) (100%, 0%, 0%, 90%)
(180, 0%, 0%) (0%, 0%, 0%, 100%)	(180, 0%, 50%) (0%, 0%, 0%, 50%)	(180, 100%, 0%) (0%, 0%, 0%, 100%)

H = 185, S = 100%, L = X%	H = 185, S = X%, L = 50%	H = 185, S = X%, L = X%
(185, 100%, 100%) (0%, 0%, 0%, 0%)	(185, 100%, 50%) (100%, 8%, 0%, 0%)	(185, 100%, 100%) (0%, 0%, 0%, 0%)
(185, 100%, 95%) (10%, 1%, 0%, 0%)	(185, 95%, 50%) (97%, 8%, 0%, 3%)	(185, 95%, 95%) (10%, 1%, 0%, 0%)
(185, 100%, 90%) (20%, 2%, 0%, 0%)	(185, 90%, 50%) (95%, 8%, 0%, 5%)	(185, 90%, 90%) (18%, 2%, 0%, 1%)
(185, 100%, 85%) (30%, 3%, 0%, 0%)	(185, 85%, 50%) (92%, 8%, 0%, 7%)	(185, 85%, 85%) (26%, 2%, 0%, 2%)
(185, 100%, 80%) (40%, 3%, 0%, 0%)	(185, 80%, 50%) (89%, 7%, 0%, 10%)	(185, 80%, 80%) (33%, 3%, 0%, 4%)
(185, 100%, 75%) (50%, 4%, 0%, 0%)	(185, 75%, 50%) (86%, 7%, 0%, 13%)	(185, 75%, 75%) (40%, 3%, 0%, 6%)
(185, 100%, 70%) (60%, 5%, 0%, 0%)	(185, 70%, 50%) (82%, 7%, 0%, 15%)	(185, 70%, 70%) (46%, 4%, 0%, 9%)
(185, 100%, 65%) (70%, 6%, 0%, 0%)	(185, 65%, 50%) (79%, 7%, 0%, 18%)	(185, 65%, 65%) (52%, 4%, 0%, 12%)
(185, 100%, 60%) (80%, 7%, 0%, 0%)	(185, 60%, 50%) (75%, 6%, 0%, 20%)	(185, 60%, 60%) (57%, 5%, 0%, 16%)
(185, 100%, 55%) (90%, 8%, 0%, 0%)	(185, 55%, 50%) (71%, 6%, 0%, 22%)	(185, 55%, 55%) (62%, 5%, 0%, 20%)
(185, 100%, 50%) (100%, 8%, 0%, 0%)	(185, 50%, 50%) (67%, 6%, 0%, 25%)	(185, 50%, 50%) (67%, 6%, 0%, 25%)
(185, 100%, 45%) (100%, 8%, 0%, 10%)	(185, 45%, 50%) (62%, 5%, 0%, 28%)	(185, 45%, 45%) (62%, 5%, 0%, 35%)
(185, 100%, 40%) (100%, 8%, 0%, 20%)	(185, 40%, 50%) (57%, 5%, 0%, 30%)	(185, 40, 40%) (57%, 5%, 0%, 44%)
(185, 100%, 35%) (100%, 8%, 0%, 30%)	(185, 35%, 50%) (52%, 4%, 0%, 32%)	(185, 35%, 35%) (52%, 4%, 0%, 53%)
(185, 100%, 30%) (100%, 8%, 0%, 40%)	(185, 30%, 50%) (46%, 4%, 0%, 35%)	(185, 30%, 30%) (46%, 4%, 0%, 61%)
(185, 100%, 25%) (100%, 8%, 0%, 50%)	(185, 25%, 50%) (40%, 3%, 0%, 38%)	(185, 25%, 25%) (40%, 3%, 0%, 69%)
(185, 100%, 20%) (100%, 8%, 0%, 60%)	(185, 20%, 50%) (33%, 3%, 0%, 40%)	(185, 20%, 20%) (33%, 3%, 0%, 76%)
(185, 100%, 15%) (100%, 8%, 0%, 70%)	(185, 15%, 50%) (26%, 2%, 0%, 43%)	(185, 15%, 15%) (26%, 2%, 0%, 83%)
(185, 100%, 10%) (100%, 8%, 0%, 80%)	(185, 10%, 50%) (18%, 2%, 0%, 45%)	(185, 10%, 10%) (18%, 2%, 0%, 89%)
(185, 100%, 5%) (100%, 8%, 0%, 90%)	(185, 5%, 50%) (10%, 1%, 0%, 47%)	(185, 5%, 5%) (10%, 1%, 0%, 95%)
(185, 100%, 0%) (0%, 0%, 0%, 100%)	(185, 0%, 50%) (0%, 0%, 0%, 50%)	(185, 0%, 0%) (0%, 0%, 0%, 100%)

H = 190, S = X%, L = X%	H = 190, S = X%, L = 50%	H = 190, S = 100%, L = X%
(190, 100%, 100%) (0%, 0%, 0%, 0%)	(190, 100%, 50%) (100%, 17%, 0%, 0%)	(190, 100%, 100%) (0%, 0%, 0%, 0%)
(190, 95%, 95%) (10%, 2%, 0%, 0%)	(190, 95%, 50%) (97%, 16%, 0%, 3%)	(190, 100%, 95%) (10%, 2%, 0%, 0%)
(190, 90%, 90%) (18%, 3%, 0%, 1%)	(190, 90%, 50%) (95%, 16%, 0%, 5%)	(190, 100%, 90%) (20%, 3%, 0%, 0%)
(190, 85%, 85%) (26%, 4%, 0%, 2%)	(190, 85%, 50%) (92%, 15%, 0%, 7%)	(190, 100%, 85%) (30%, 5%, 0%, 0%)
(190, 80%, 80%) (33%, 6%, 0%, 4%)	(190, 80%, 50%) (89%, 15%, 0%, 10%)	(190, 100%, 80%) (40%, 7%, 0%, 0%)
(190, 75%, 75%) (40%, 7%, 0%, 6%)	(190, 75%, 50%) (86%, 14%, 0%, 13%)	(190, 100%, 75%) (50%, 8%, 0%, 0%)
(190, 70%, 70%) (46%, 8%, 0%, 9%)	(190, 70%, 50%) (82%, 14%, 0%, 15%)	(190, 100%, 70%) (60%, 10%, 0%, 0%)
(190, 65%, 65%) (52%, 9%, 0%, 12%)	(190, 65%, 50%) (79%, 13%, 0%, 18%)	(190, 100%, 65%) (70%, 12%, 0%, 0%)
(190, 60%, 60%) (57%, 10%, 0%, 16%)	(190, 60%, 50%) (75%, 12%, 0%, 20%)	(190, 100%, 60%) (80%, 13%, 0%, 0%)
(190, 55%, 55%) (62%, 10%, 0%, 20%)	(190, 55%, 50%) (71%, 12%, 0%, 22%)	(190, 100%, 55%) (90%, 15%, 0%, 0%)
(190, 50%, 50%) (67%, 11%, 0%, 25%)	(190, 50%, 50%) (67%, 11%, 0%, 25%)	(190, 100%, 50%) (100%, 17%, 0%, 0%)
(190, 45%, 45%) (62%, 10%, 0%, 35%)	(190, 45%, 50%) (62%, 10%, 0%, 28%)	(190, 100%, 45%) (100%, 17%, 0%, 10%)
(190, 40, 40%) (57%, 10%, 0%, 44%)	(190, 40%, 50%) (57%, 10%, 0%, 30%)	(190, 100%, 40%) (100%, 17%, 0%, 20%)
(190, 35%, 35%) (52%, 9%, 0%, 53%)	(190, 35%, 50%) (52%, 9%, 0%, 32%)	(190, 100%, 35%) (100%, 17%, 0%, 30%)
(190, 30%, 30%) (46%, 8%, 0%, 61%)	(190, 30%, 50%) (46%, 8%, 0%, 35%)	(190, 100%, 30%) (100%, 17%, 0%, 40%)
(190, 25%, 25%) (40%, 7%, 0%, 69%)	(190, 25%, 50%) (40%, 7%, 0%, 38%)	(190, 100%, 25%) (100%, 17%, 0%, 50%)
(190, 20%, 20%) (33%, 6%, 0%, 76%)	(190, 20%, 50%) (33%, 6%, 0%, 40%)	(190, 100%, 20%) (100%, 17%, 0%, 60%)
(190, 15%, 15%) (26%, 4%, 0%, 83%)	(190, 15%, 50%) (26%, 4%, 0%, 43%)	(190, 100%, 15%) (100%, 17%, 0%, 70%)
(190, 10%, 10%) (18%, 3%, 0%, 89%)	(190, 10%, 50%) (18%, 3%, 0%, 45%)	(190, 100%, 10%) (100%, 17%, 0%, 80%)
(190, 5%, 5%) (10%, 2%, 0%, 95%)	(190, 5%, 50%) (10%, 2%, 0%, 47%)	(190, 100%, 5%) (100%, 17%, 0%, 90%)
(190, 0%, 0%) (0%, 0%, 0%, 100%)	(190, 0%, 50%) (0%, 0%, 0%, 50%)	(190, 100%, 0%) (0%, 0%, 0%, 100%)

H = 195, S = 100%, L = X%	H = 195, S = X%, L = 50%	H = 195, S = X%, L = X%
(195, 100%, 100%) (0%, 0%, 0%, 0%)	(195, 100%, 50%) (100%, 25%, 0%, 0%)	(195, 100%, 100%) (0%, 0%, 0%, 0%)
(195, 100%, 95%) (10%, 3%, 0%, 0%)	(195, 95%, 50%) (97%, 24%, 0%, 3%)	(195, 95%, 95%) (10%, 2%, 0%, 0%)
(195, 100%, 90%) (20%, 5%, 0%, 0%)	(195, 90%, 50%) (95%, 24%, 0%, 5%)	(195, 90%, 90%) (18%, 5%, 0%, 1%)
(195, 100%, 85%) (30%, 7%, 0%, 0%)	(195, 85%, 50%) (92%, 23%, 0%, 7%)	(195, 85%, 85%) (26%, 7%, 0%, 2%)
(195, 100%, 80%) (40%, 10%, 0%, 0%)	(195, 80%, 50%) (89%, 22%, 0%, 10%)	(195, 80%, 80%) (33%, 8%, 0%, 4%)
(195, 100%, 75%) (50%, 13%, 0%, 0%)	(195, 75%, 50%) (86%, 21%, 0%, 13%)	(195, 75%, 75%) (40%, 10%, 0%, 6%)
(195, 100%, 70%) (60%, 15%, 0%, 0%)	(195, 70%, 50%) (82%, 21%, 0%, 15%)	(195, 70%, 70%) (46%, 12%, 0%, 9%)
(195, 100%, 65%) (70%, 17%, 0%, 0%)	(195, 65%, 50%) (79%, 20%, 0%, 18%)	(195, 65%, 65%) (52%, 13%, 0%, 12%)
(195, 100%, 60%) (80%, 20%, 0%, 0%)	(195, 60%, 50%) (75%, 19%, 0%, 20%)	(195, 60%, 60%) (57%, 14%, 0%, 16%)
(195, 100%, 55%) (90%, 22%, 0%, 0%)	(195, 55%, 50%) (71%, 18%, 0%, 22%)	(195, 55%, 55%) (62%, 16%, 0%, 20%)
(195, 100%, 50%) (100%, 25%, 0%, 0%)	(195, 50%, 50%) (67%, 17%, 0%, 25%)	(195, 50%, 50%) (67%, 17%, 0%, 25%)
(195, 100%, 45%) (100%, 25%, 0%, 10%)	(195, 45%, 50%) (62%, 16%, 0%, 28%)	(195, 45%, 45%) (62%, 16%, 0%, 35%)
(195, 100%, 40%) (100%, 25%, 0%, 20%)	(195, 40%, 50%) (57%, 14%, 0%, 30%)	(195, 40, 40%) (57%, 14%, 0%, 44%)
(195, 100%, 35%) (100%, 25%, 0%, 30%)	(195, 35%, 50%) (52%, 13%, 0%, 32%)	(195, 35%, 35%) (52%, 13%, 0%, 53%)
(195, 100%, 30%) (100%, 25%, 0%, 40%)	(195, 30%, 50%) (46%, 12%, 0%, 35%)	(195, 30%, 30%) (46%, 12%, 0%, 61%)
(195, 100%, 25%) (100%, 25%, 0%, 50%)	(195, 25%, 50%) (40%, 10%, 0%, 38%)	(195, 25%, 25%) (40%, 10%, 0%, 69%)
(195, 100%, 20%) (100%, 25%, 0%, 60%)	(195, 20%, 50%) (33%, 8%, 0%, 40%)	(195, 20%, 20%) (33%, 8%, 0%, 76%)
(195, 100%, 15%) (100%, 25%, 0%, 70%)	(195, 15%, 50%) (26%, 7%, 0%, 43%)	(195, 15%, 15%) (26%, 7%, 0%, 83%)
(195, 100%, 10%) (100%, 25%, 0%, 80%)	(195, 10%, 50%) (18%, 5%, 0%, 45%)	(195, 10%, 10%) (18%, 5%, 0%, 89%)
(195, 100%, 5%) (100%, 25%, 0%, 90%)	(195, 5%, 50%) (10%, 2%, 0%, 47%)	(195, 5%, 5%) (10%, 2%, 0%, 95%)
(195, 100%, 0%) (0%, 0%, 0%, 100%)	(195, 0%, 50%) (0%, 0%, 0%, 50%)	(195, 0%, 0%) (0%, 0%, 0%, 100%)

H = 200, S = X%, L = X%	H = 200, S = X%, L = 50%	H = 200, S = 100%, L = X%
(200, 100%, 100%) (0%, 0%, 0%, 0%)	(200, 100%, 50%) (100%, 33%, 0%, 0%)	(200, 100%, 100%) (0%, 0%, 0%, 0%)
(200, 95%, 95%) (10%, 3%, 0%, 0%)	(200, 95%, 50%) (97%, 32%, 0%, 3%)	(200, 100%, 95%) (10%, 3%, 0%, 0%)
(200, 90%, 90%) (18%, 6%, 0%, 1%)	(200, 90%, 50%) (95%, 32%, 0%, 5%)	(200, 100%, 90%) (20%, 7%, 0%, 0%)
(200, 85%, 85%) (26%, 9%, 0%, 2%)	(200, 85%, 50%) (92%, 31%, 0%, 7%)	(200, 100%, 85%) (30%, 10%, 0%, 0%)
(200, 80%, 80%) (33%, 11%, 0%, 4%)	(200, 80%, 50%) (89%, 30%, 0%, 10%)	(200, 100%, 80%) (40%, 13%, 0%, 0%)
(200, 75%, 75%) (40%, 13%, 0%, 6%)	(200, 75%, 50%) (86%, 29%, 0%, 13%)	(200, 100%, 75%) (50%, 17%, 0%, 0%)
(200, 70%, 70%) (46%, 15%, 0%, 9%)	(200, 70%, 50%) (82%, 27%, 0%, 15%)	(200, 100%, 70%) (60%, 20%, 0%, 0%)
(200, 65%, 65%) (52%, 17%, 0%, 12%)	(200, 65%, 50%) (79%, 26%, 0%, 18%)	(200, 100%, 65%) (70%, 23%, 0%, 0%)
(200, 60%, 60%) (57%, 19%, 0%, 16%)	(200, 60%, 50%) (75%, 25%, 0%, 20%)	(200, 100%, 60%) (80%, 27%, 0%, 0%)
(200, 55%, 55%) (62%, 21%, 0%, 20%)	(200, 55%, 50%) (71%, 24%, 0%, 22%)	(200, 100%, 55%) (90%, 30%, 0%, 0%)
(200, 50%, 50%) (67%, 22%, 0%, 25%)	(200, 50%, 50%) (67%, 22%, 0%, 25%)	(200, 100%, 50%) (100%, 33%, 0%, 0%)
(200, 45%, 45%) (62%, 21%, 0%, 35%)	(200, 45%, 50%) (62%, 21%, 0%, 28%)	(200, 100%, 45%) (100%, 33%, 0%, 10%)
(200, 40, 40%) (57%, 19%, 0%, 44%)	(200, 40%, 50%) (57%, 19%, 0%, 30%)	(200, 100%, 40%) (100%, 33%, 0%, 20%)
(200, 35%, 35%) (52%, 17%, 0%, 53%)	(200, 35%, 50%) (52%, 17%, 0%, 32%)	(200, 100%, 35%) (100%, 33%, 0%, 30%)
(200, 30%, 30%) (46%, 15%, 0%, 61%)	(200, 30%, 50%) (46%, 15%, 0%, 35%)	(200, 100%, 30%) (100%, 33%, 0%, 40%)
(200, 25%, 25%) (40%, 13%, 0%, 69%)	(200, 25%, 50%) (40%, 13%, 0%, 38%)	(200, 100%, 25%) (100%, 33%, 0%, 50%)
(200, 20%, 20%) (33%, 11%, 0%, 76%)	(200, 20%, 50%) (33%, 11%, 0%, 40%)	(200, 100%, 20%) (100%, 33%, 0%, 60%)
(200, 15%, 15%) (26%, 9%, 0%, 83%)	(200, 15%, 50%) (26%, 9%, 0%, 43%)	(200, 100%, 15%) (100%, 33%, 0%, 70%)
(200, 10%, 10%) (18%, 6%, 0%, 89%)	(200, 10%, 50%) (18%, 6%, 0%, 45%)	(200, 100%, 10%) (100%, 33%, 0%, 80%)
(200, 5%, 5%) (10%, 3%, 0%, 95%)	(200, 5%, 50%) (10%, 3%, 0%, 47%)	(200, 100%, 5%) (100%, 33%, 0%, 90%)
(200, 0%, 0%) (0%, 0%, 0%, 100%)	(200, 0%, 50%) (0%, 0%, 0%, 50%)	(200, 100%, 0%) (0%, 0%, 0%, 100%)

H = 205, S = 100%, L = X%	H = 205, S = X%, L = 50%	H = 205, S = X%, L = X%
(205, 100%, 100%) (0%, 0%, 0%, 0%)	(205, 100%, 50%) (100%, 42%, 0%, 0%)	(205, 100%, 100%) (0%, 0%, 0%, 0%)
(205, 100%, 95%) (10%, 4%, 0%, 0%)	(205, 95%, 50%) (97%, 41%, 0%, 3%)	(205, 95%, 95%) (10%, 4%, 0%, 0%)
(205, 100%, 90%) (20%, 8%, 0%, 0%)	(205, 90%, 50%) (95%, 39%, 0%, 5%)	(205, 90%, 90%) (18%, 8%, 0%, 1%)
(205, 100%, 85%) (30%, 13%, 0%, 0%)	(205, 85%, 50%) (92%, 38%, 0%, 7%)	(205, 85%, 85%) (26%, 11%, 0%, 2%)
(205, 100%, 80%) (40%, 17%, 0%, 0%)	(205, 80%, 50%) (89%, 37%, 0%, 10%)	(205, 80%, 80%) (33%, 14%, 0%, 4%)
(205, 100%, 75%) (50%, 21%, 0%, 0%)	(205, 75%, 50%) (86%, 36%, 0%, 13%)	(205, 75%, 75%) (40%, 17%, 0%, 6%)
(205, 100%, 70%) (60%, 25%, 0%, 0%)	(205, 70%, 50%) (82%, 34%, 0%, 15%)	(205, 70%, 70%) (46%, 19%, 0%, 9%)
(205, 100%, 65%) (70%, 29%, 0%, 0%)	(205, 65%, 50%) (79%, 33%, 0%, 18%)	(205, 65%, 65%) (52%, 22%, 0%, 12%)
(205, 100%, 60%) (80%, 33%, 0%, 0%)	(205, 60%, 50%) (75%, 31%, 0%, 20%)	(205, 60%, 60%) (57%, 24%, 0%, 16%)
(205, 100%, 55%) (90%, 37%, 0%, 0%)	(205, 55%, 50%) (71%, 30%, 0%, 22%)	(205, 55%, 55%) (62%, 26%, 0%, 20%)
(205, 100%, 50%) (100%, 42%, 0%, 0%)	(205, 50%, 50%) (67%, 28%, 0%, 25%)	(205, 50%, 50%) (67%, 28%, 0%, 25%)
(205, 100%, 45%) (100%, 42%, 0%, 10%)	(205, 45%, 50%) (62%, 26%, 0%, 28%)	(205, 45%, 45%) (62%, 26%, 0%, 35%)
(205, 100%, 40%) (100%, 42%, 0%, 20%)	(205, 40%, 50%) (57%, 24%, 0%, 30%)	(205, 40, 40%) (57%, 24%, 0%, 44%)
(205, 100%, 35%) (100%, 42%, 0%, 30%)	(205, 35%, 50%) (52%, 22%, 0%, 32%)	(205, 35%, 35%) (52%, 22%, 0%, 53%)
(205, 100%, 30%) (100%, 42%, 0%, 40%)	(205, 30%, 50%) (46%, 19%, 0%, 35%)	(205, 30%, 30%) (46%, 19%, 0%, 61%)
(205, 100%, 25%) (100%, 42%, 0%, 50%)	(205, 25%, 50%) (40%, 17%, 0%, 38%)	(205, 25%, 25%) (40%, 17%, 0%, 69%)
(205, 100%, 20%) (100%, 42%, 0%, 60%)	(205, 20%, 50%) (33%, 14%, 0%, 40%)	(205, 20%, 20%) (33%, 14%, 0%, 76%)
(205, 100%, 15%) (100%, 42%, 0%, 70%)	(205, 15%, 50%) (26%, 11%, 0%, 43%)	(205, 15%, 15%) (26%, 11%, 0%, 83%)
(205, 100%, 10%) (100%, 42%, 0%, 80%)	(205, 10%, 50%) (18%, 8%, 0%, 45%)	(205, 10%, 10%) (18%, 8%, 0%, 89%)
(205, 100%, 5%) (100%, 42%, 0%, 90%)	(205, 5%, 50%) (10%, 4%, 0%, 47%)	(205, 5%, 5%) (10%, 4%, 0%, 95%)
(205, 100%, 0%) (0%, 0%, 0%, 100%)	(205, 0%, 50%) (0%, 0%, 0%, 50%)	(205, 0%, 0%) (0%, 0%, 0%, 100%)

H = 210, S = X%, L = X%	H = 210, S = X%, L = 50%	H = 210, S = 100%, L = X%
(210, 100%, 100%) (0%, 0%, 0%, 0%)	(210, 100%, 50%) (100%, 50%, 0%, 0%)	(210, 100%, 100%) (0%, 0%, 0%, 0%)
(210, 95%, 95%) (10%, 5%, 0%, 0%)	(210, 95%, 50%) (97%, 49%, 0%, 3%)	(210, 100%, 95%) (10%, 5%, 0%, 0%)
(210, 90%, 90%) (18%, 9%, 0%, 1%)	(210, 90%, 50%) (95%, 47%, 0%, 5%)	(210, 100%, 90%) (20%, 10%, 0%, 0%)
(210, 85%, 85%) (26%, 13%, 0%, 2%)	(210, 85%, 50%) (92%, 46%, 0%, 7%)	(210, 100%, 85%) (30%, 15%, 0%, 0%)
(210, 80%, 80%) (33%, 17%, 0%, 4%)	(210, 80%, 50%) (89%, 44%, 0%, 10%)	(210, 100%, 80%) (40%, 20%, 0%, 0%)
(210, 75%, 75%) (40%, 20%, 0%, 6%)	(210, 75%, 50%) (86%, 43%, 0%, 13%)	(210, 100%, 75%) (50%, 25%, 0%, 0%)
(210, 70%, 70%) (46%, 23%, 0%, 9%)	(210, 70%, 50%) (82%, 41%, 0%, 15%)	(210, 100%, 70%) (60%, 30%, 0%, 0%)
(210, 65%, 65%) (52%, 26%, 0%, 12%)	(210, 65%, 50%) (79%, 39%, 0%, 18%)	(210, 100%, 65%) (70%, 35%, 0%, 0%)
(210, 60%, 60%) (57%, 29%, 0%, 16%)	(210, 60%, 50%) (75%, 38%, 0%, 20%)	(210, 100%, 60%) (80%, 40%, 0%, 0%)
(210, 55%, 55%) (62%, 31%, 0%, 20%)	(210, 55%, 50%) (71%, 35%, 0%, 22%)	(210, 100%, 55%) (90%, 45%, 0%, 0%)
(210, 50%, 50%) (67%, 33%, 0%, 25%)	(210, 50%, 50%) (67%, 33%, 0%, 25%)	(210, 100%, 50%) (100%, 50%, 0%, 0%)
(210, 45%, 45%) (62%, 31%, 0%, 35%)	(210, 45%, 50%) (62%, 31%, 0%, 28%)	(210, 100%, 45%) (100%, 50%, 0%, 10%)
(210, 40, 40%) (57%, 29%, 0%, 44%)	(210, 40%, 50%) (57%, 29%, 0%, 30%)	(210, 100%, 40%) (100%, 50%, 0%, 20%)
(210, 35%, 35%) (52%, 26%, 0%, 53%)	(210, 35%, 50%) (52%, 26%, 0%, 32%)	(210, 100%, 35%) (100%, 50%, 0%, 30%)
(210, 30%, 30%) (46%, 23%, 0%, 61%)	(210, 30%, 50%) (46%, 23%, 0%, 35%)	(210, 100%, 30%) (100%, 50%, 0%, 40%)
(210, 25%, 25%) (40%, 20%, 0%, 69%)	(210, 25%, 50%) (40%, 20%, 0%, 38%)	(210, 100%, 25%) (100%, 50%, 0%, 50%)
(210, 20%, 20%) (33%, 17%, 0%, 76%)	(210, 20%, 50%) (33%, 17%, 0%, 40%)	(210, 100%, 20%) (100%, 50%, 0%, 60%)
(210, 15%, 15%) (26%, 13%, 0%, 83%)	(210, 15%, 50%) (26%, 13%, 0%, 43%)	(210, 100%, 15%) (100%, 50%, 0%, 70%)
(210, 10%, 10%) (18%, 9%, 0%, 89%)	(210, 10%, 50%) (18%, 9%, 0%, 45%)	(210, 100%, 10%) (100%, 50%, 0%, 80%)
(210, 5%, 5%) (10%, 5%, 0%, 95%)	(210, 5%, 50%) (10%, 5%, 0%, 47%)	(210, 100%, 5%) (100%, 50%, 0%, 90%)
(210, 0%, 0%) (0%, 0%, 0%, 100%)	(210, 0%, 50%) (0%, 0%, 0%, 50%)	(210, 100%, 0%) (0%, 0%, 0%, 100%)

H = 215, S = 100%, L = X%	H = 215, S = X%, L = 50%	H = 215, S = X%, L = X%
(215, 100%, 100%) (0%, 0%, 0%, 0%)	(215, 100%, 50%) (100%, 58%, 0%, 0%)	(215, 100%, 100%) (0%, 0%, 0%, 0%)
(215, 100%, 95%) (10%, 6%, 0%, 0%)	(215, 95%, 50%) (97%, 57%, 0%, 3%)	(215, 95%, 95%) (10%, 6%, 0%, 0%)
(215, 100%, 90%) (20%, 12%, 0%, 0%)	(215, 90%, 50%) (95%, 55%, 0%, 5%)	(215, 90%, 90%) (18%, 11%, 0%, 1%)
(215, 100%, 85%) (30%, 18%, 0%, 0%)	(215, 85%, 50%) (92%, 54%, 0%, 7%)	(215, 85%, 85%) (26%, 15%, 0%, 2%)
(215, 100%, 80%) (40%, 23%, 0%, 0%)	(215, 80%, 50%) (89%, 52%, 0%, 10%)	(215, 80%, 80%) (33%, 19%, 0%, 4%)
(215, 100%, 75%) (50%, 29%, 0%, 0%)	(215, 75%, 50%) (86%, 50%, 0%, 13%)	(215, 75%, 75%) (40%, 23%, 0%, 6%)
(215, 100%, 70%) (60%, 35%, 0%, 0%)	(215, 70%, 50%) (82%, 48%, 0%, 15%)	(215, 70%, 70%) (46%, 27%, 0%, 9%)
(215, 100%, 65%) (70%, 41%, 0%, 0%)	(215, 65%, 50%) (79%, 46%, 0%, 18%)	(215, 65%, 65%) (52%, 30%, 0%, 12%)
(215, 100%, 60%) (80%, 47%, 0%, 0%)	(215, 60%, 50%) (75%, 44%, 0%, 20%)	(215, 60%, 60%) (57%, 33%, 0%, 16%)
(215, 100%, 55%) (90%, 53%, 0%, 0%)	(215, 55%, 50%) (71%, 41%, 0%, 22%)	(215, 55%, 55%) (62%, 36%, 0%, 20%)
(215, 100%, 50%) (100%, 58%, 0%, 0%)	(215, 50%, 50%) (67%, 39%, 0%, 25%)	(215, 50%, 50%) (67%, 39%, 0%, 25%)
(215, 100%, 45%) (100%, 58%, 0%, 10%)	(215, 45%, 50%) (62%, 36%, 0%, 28%)	(215, 45%, 45%) (62%, 36%, 0%, 35%)
(215, 100%, 40%) (100%, 58%, 0%, 20%)	(215, 40%, 50%) (57%, 33%, 0%, 30%)	(215, 40, 40%) (57%, 33%, 0%, 44%)
(215, 100%, 35%) (100%, 58%, 0%, 30%)	(215, 35%, 50%) (52%, 30%, 0%, 32%)	(215, 35%, 35%) (52%, 30%, 0%, 53%)
(215, 100%, 30%) (100%, 58%, 0%, 40%)	(215, 30%, 50%) (46%, 27%, 0%, 35%)	(215, 30%, 30%) (46%, 27%, 0%, 61%)
(215, 100%, 25%) (100%, 58%, 0%, 50%)	(215, 25%, 50%) (40%, 23%, 0%, 38%)	(215, 25%, 25%) (40%, 23%, 0%, 69%)
(215, 100%, 20%) (100%, 58%, 0%, 60%)	(215, 20%, 50%) (33%, 19%, 0%, 40%)	(215, 20%, 20%) (33%, 19%, 0%, 76%)
(215, 100%, 15%) (100%, 58%, 0%, 70%)	(215, 15%, 50%) (26%, 15%, 0%, 43%)	(215, 15%, 15%) (26%, 15%, 0%, 83%)
(215, 100%, 10%) (100%, 58%, 0%, 80%)	(215, 10%, 50%) (18%, 11%, 0%, 45%)	(215, 10%, 10%) (18%, 11%, 0%, 89%)
(215, 100%, 5%) (100%, 58%, 0%, 90%)	(215, 5%, 50%) (10%, 6%, 0%, 47%)	(215, 5%, 5%) (10%, 6%, 0%, 95%)
(215, 100%, 0%) (0%, 0%, 0%, 100%)	(215, 0%, 50%) (0%, 0%, 0%, 50%)	(215, 0%, 0%) (0%, 0%, 0%, 100%)

H = 220, S = X%, L = X%	H = 220, S = X%, L = 50%	H = 220, S = 100%, L = X%
(220, 100%, 100%) (0%, 0%, 0%, 0%)	(220, 100%, 50%) (100%, 67%, 0%, 0%)	(220, 100%, 100%) (0%, 0%, 0%, 0%)
(220, 95%, 95%) (10%, 6%, 0%, 0%)	(220, 95%, 50%) (97%, 65%, 0%, 3%)	(220, 100%, 95%) (10%, 7%, 0%, 0%)
(220, 90%, 90%) (18%, 12%, 0%, 1%)	(220, 90%, 50%) (95%, 63%, 0%, 5%)	(220, 100%, 90%) (20%, 13%, 0%, 0%)
(220, 85%, 85%) (26%, 17%, 0%, 2%)	(220, 85%, 50%) (92%, 61%, 0%, 7%)	(220, 100%, 85%) (30%, 20%, 0%, 0%)
(220, 80%, 80%) (33%, 22%, 0%, 4%)	(220, 80%, 50%) (89%, 59%, 0%, 10%)	(220, 100%, 80%) (40%, 27%, 0%, 0%)
(220, 75%, 75%) (40%, 27%, 0%, 6%)	(220, 75%, 50%) (86%, 57%, 0%, 13%)	(220, 100%, 75%) (50%, 33%, 0%, 0%)
(220, 70%, 70%) (46%, 31%, 0%, 9%)	(220, 70%, 50%) (82%, 55%, 0%, 15%)	(220, 100%, 70%) (60%, 40%, 0%, 0%)
(220, 65%, 65%) (52%, 35%, 0%, 12%)	(220, 65%, 50%) (79%, 53%, 0%, 18%)	(220, 100%, 65%) (70%, 47%, 0%, 0%)
(220, 60%, 60%) (57%, 38%, 0%, 16%)	(220, 60%, 50%) (75%, 50%, 0%, 20%)	(220, 100%, 60%) (80%, 53%, 0%, 0%)
(220, 55%, 55%) (62%, 41%, 0%, 20%)	(220, 55%, 50%) (71%, 47%, 0%, 22%)	(220, 100%, 55%) (90%, 60%, 0%, 0%)
(220, 50%, 50%) (67%, 44%, 0%, 25%)	(220, 50%, 50%) (67%, 44%, 0%, 25%)	(220, 100%, 50%) (100%, 67%, 0%, 0%)
(220, 45%, 45%) (62%, 41%, 0%, 35%)	(220, 45%, 50%) (62%, 41%, 0%, 28%)	(220, 100%, 45%) (100%, 67%, 0%, 10%)
(220, 40, 40%) (57%, 38%, 0%, 44%)	(220, 40%, 50%) (57%, 38%, 0%, 30%)	(220, 100%, 40%) (100%, 67%, 0%, 20%)
(220, 35%, 35%) (52%, 35%, 0%, 53%)	(220, 35%, 50%) (52%, 35%, 0%, 32%)	(220, 100%, 35%) (100%, 67%, 0%, 30%)
(220, 30%, 30%) (46%, 31%, 0%, 61%)	(220, 30%, 50%) (46%, 31%, 0%, 35%)	(220, 100%, 30%) (100%, 67%, 0%, 40%)
(220, 25%, 25%) (40%, 27%, 0%, 69%)	(220, 25%, 50%) (40%, 27%, 0%, 38%)	(220, 100%, 25%) (100%, 67%, 0%, 50%)
(220, 20%, 20%) (33%, 22%, 0%, 76%)	(220, 20%, 50%) (33%, 22%, 0%, 40%)	(220, 100%, 20%) (100%, 67%, 0%, 60%)
(220, 15%, 15%) (26%, 17%, 0%, 83%)	(220, 15%, 50%) (26%, 17%, 0%, 43%)	(220, 100%, 15%) (100%, 67%, 0%, 70%)
(220, 10%, 10%) (18%, 12%, 0%, 89%)	(220, 10%, 50%) (18%, 12%, 0%, 45%)	(220, 100%, 10%) (100%, 67%, 0%, 80%)
(220, 5%, 5%) (10%, 6%, 0%, 95%)	(220, 5%, 50%) (10%, 6%, 0%, 47%)	(220, 100%, 5%) (100%, 67%, 0%, 90%)
(220, 0%, 0%) (0%, 0%, 0%, 100%)	(220, 0%, 50%) (0%, 0%, 0%, 50%)	(220, 100%, 0%) (0%, 0%, 0%, 100%)

H = 225, S = 100%, L = X%	H = 225, S = X%, L = 50%	H = 225, S = X%, L = X%
(225, 100%, 100%) (0%, 0%, 0%, 0%)	(225, 100%, 50%) (100%, 75%, 0%, 0%)	(225, 100%, 100%) (0%, 0%, 0%, 0%)
(225, 100%, 95%) (10%, 8%, 0%, 0%)	(225, 95%, 50%) (97%, 73%, 0%, 3%)	(225, 95%, 95%) (10%, 7%, 0%, 0%)
(225, 100%, 90%) (20%, 15%, 0%, 0%)	(225, 90%, 50%) (95%, 71%, 0%, 5%)	(225, 90%, 90%) (18%, 14%, 0%, 1%)
(225, 100%, 85%) (30%, 23%, 0%, 0%)	(225, 85%, 50%) (92%, 69%, 0%, 7%)	(225, 85%, 85%) (26%, 20%, 0%, 2%)
(225, 100%, 80%) (40%, 30%, 0%, 0%)	(225, 80%, 50%) (89%, 67%, 0%, 10%)	(225, 80%, 80%) (33%, 25%, 0%, 4%)
(225, 100%, 75%) (50%, 38%, 0%, 0%)	(225, 75%, 50%) (86%, 64%, 0%, 13%)	(225, 75%, 75%) (40%, 30%, 0%, 6%)
(225, 100%, 70%) (60%, 45%, 0%, 0%)	(225, 70%, 50%) (82%, 62%, 0%, 15%)	(225, 70%, 70%) (46%, 35%, 0%, 9%)
(225, 100%, 65%) (70%, 52%, 0%, 0%)	(225, 65%, 50%) (79%, 59%, 0%, 18%)	(225, 65%, 65%) (52%, 39%, 0%, 12%)
(225, 100%, 60%) (80%, 60%, 0%, 0%)	(225, 60%, 50%) (75%, 56%, 0%, 20%)	(225, 60%, 60%) (57%, 43%, 0%, 16%)
(225, 100%, 55%) (90%, 67%, 0%, 0%)	(225, 55%, 50%) (71%, 53%, 0%, 22%)	(225, 55%, 55%) (62%, 47%, 0%, 20%)
(225, 100%, 50%) (100%, 75%, 0%, 0%)	(225, 50%, 50%) (67%, 50%, 0%, 25%)	(225, 50%, 50%) (67%, 50%, 0%, 25%)
(225, 100%, 45%) (100%, 75%, 0%, 10%)	(225, 45%, 50%) (62%, 47%, 0%, 28%)	(225, 45%, 45%) (62%, 47%, 0%, 35%)
(225, 100%, 40%) (100%, 75%, 0%, 20%)	(225, 40%, 50%) (57%, 43%, 0%, 30%)	(225, 40, 40%) (57%, 43%, 0%, 44%)
(225, 100%, 35%) (100%, 75%, 0%, 30%)	(225, 35%, 50%) (52%, 39%, 0%, 32%)	(225, 35%, 35%) (52%, 39%, 0%, 53%)
(225, 100%, 30%) (100%, 75%, 0%, 40%)	(225, 30%, 50%) (46%, 35%, 0%, 35%)	(225, 30%, 30%) (46%, 35%, 0%, 61%)
(225, 100%, 25%) (100%, 75%, 0%, 50%)	(225, 25%, 50%) (40%, 30%, 0%, 38%)	(225, 25%, 25%) (40%, 30%, 0%, 69%)
(225, 100%, 20%) (100%, 75%, 0%, 60%)	(225, 20%, 50%) (33%, 25%, 0%, 40%)	(225, 20%, 20%) (33%, 25%, 0%, 76%)
(225, 100%, 15%) (100%, 75%, 0%, 70%)	(225, 15%, 50%) (26%, 20%, 0%, 43%)	(225, 15%, 15%) (26%, 20%, 0%, 83%)
(225, 100%, 10%) (100%, 75%, 0%, 80%)	(225, 10%, 50%) (18%, 14%, 0%, 45%)	(225, 10%, 10%) (18%, 14%, 0%, 89%)
(225, 100%, 5%) (100%, 75%, 0%, 90%)	(225, 5%, 50%) (10%, 7%, 0%, 47%)	(225, 5%, 5%) (10%, 7%, 0%, 95%)
(225, 100%, 0%) (0%, 0%, 0%, 100%)	(225, 0%, 50%) (0%, 0%, 0%, 50%)	(225, 0%, 0%) (0%, 0%, 0%, 100%)

H = 230, S = X%, L = X%	H = 230, S = X%, L = 50%	H = 230, S = 100%, L = X%
(230, 100%, 100%) (0%, 0%, 0%, 0%)	(230, 100%, 50%) (100%, 83%, 0%, 0%)	(230, 100%, 100%) (0%, 0%, 0%, 0%)
(230, 95%, 95%) (10%, 8%, 0%, 0%)	(230, 95%, 50%) (97%, 81%, 0%, 3%)	(230, 100%, 95%) (10%, 8%, 0%, 0%)
(230, 90%, 90%) (18%, 15%, 0%, 1%)	(230, 90%, 50%) (95%, 79%, 0%, 5%)	(230, 100%, 90%) (20%, 17%, 0%, 0%)
(230, 85%, 85%) (26%, 22%, 0%, 2%)	(230, 85%, 50%) (92%, 77%, 0%, 7%)	(230, 100%, 85%) (30%, 25%, 0%, 0%)
(230, 80%, 80%) (33%, 28%, 0%, 4%)	(230, 80%, 50%) (89%, 74%, 0%, 10%)	(230, 100%, 80%) (40%, 33%, 0%, 0%)
(230, 75%, 75%) (40%, 33%, 0%, 6%)	(230, 75%, 50%) (86%, 71%, 0%, 13%)	(230, 100%, 75%) (50%, 42%, 0%, 0%)
(230, 70%, 70%) (46%, 38%, 0%, 9%)	(230, 70%, 50%) (82%, 69%, 0%, 15%)	(230, 100%, 70%) (60%, 50%, 0%, 0%)
(230, 65%, 65%) (52%, 43%, 0%, 12%)	(230, 65%, 50%) (79%, 66%, 0%, 18%)	(230, 100%, 65%) (70%, 58%, 0%, 0%)
(230, 60%, 60%) (57%, 48%, 0%, 16%)	(230, 60%, 50%) (75%, 63%, 0%, 20%)	(230, 100%, 60%) (80%, 67%, 0%, 0%)
(230, 55%, 55%) (62%, 52%, 0%, 20%)	(230, 55%, 50%) (71%, 59%, 0%, 22%)	(230, 100%, 55%) (90%, 75%, 0%, 0%)
(230, 50%, 50%) (67%, 56%, 0%, 25%)	(230, 50%, 50%) (67%, 56%, 0%, 25%)	(230, 100%, 50%) (100%, 83%, 0%, 0%)
(230, 45%, 45%) (62%, 52%, 0%, 35%)	(230, 45%, 50%) (62%, 52%, 0%, 28%)	(230, 100%, 45%) (100%, 83%, 0%, 10%)
(230, 40, 40%) (57%, 48%, 0%, 44%)	(230, 40%, 50%) (57%, 48%, 0%, 30%)	(230, 100%, 40%) (100%, 83%, 0%, 20%)
(230, 35%, 35%) (52%, 43%, 0%, 53%)	(230, 35%, 50%) (52%, 43%, 0%, 32%)	(230, 100%, 35%) (100%, 83%, 0%, 30%)
(230, 30%, 30%) (46%, 38%, 0%, 61%)	(230, 30%, 50%) (46%, 38%, 0%, 35%)	(230, 100%, 30%) (100%, 83%, 0%, 40%)
(230, 25%, 25%) (40%, 33%, 0%, 69%)	(230, 25%, 50%) (40%, 33%, 0%, 38%)	(230, 100%, 25%) (100%, 83%, 0%, 50%)
(230, 20%, 20%) (33%, 28%, 0%, 76%)	(230, 20%, 50%) (33%, 28%, 0%, 40%)	(230, 100%, 20%) (100%, 83%, 0%, 60%)
(230, 15%, 15%) (26%, 22%, 0%, 83%)	(230, 15%, 50%) (26%, 22%, 0%, 43%)	(230, 100%, 15%) (100%, 83%, 0%, 70%)
(230, 10%, 10%) (18%, 15%, 0%, 89%)	(230, 10%, 50%) (18%, 15%, 0%, 45%)	(230, 100%, 10%) (100%, 83%, 0%, 80%)
(230, 5%, 5%) (10%, 8%, 0%, 95%)	(230, 5%, 50%) (10%, 8%, 0%, 47%)	(230, 100%, 5%) (100%, 83%, 0%, 90%)
(230, 0%, 0%) (0%, 0%, 0%, 100%)	(230, 0%, 50%) (0%, 0%, 0%, 50%)	(230, 100%, 0%) (0%, 0%, 0%, 100%)

H = 235, S = 100%, L = X%	H = 235, S = X%, L = 50%	H = 235, S = X%, L = X%
(235, 100%, 100%) (0%, 0%, 0%, 0%)	(235, 100%, 50%) (100%, 92%, 0%, 0%)	(235, 100%, 100%) (0%, 0%, 0%, 0%)
(235, 100%, 95%) (10%, 9%, 0%, 0%)	(235, 95%, 50%) (97%, 89%, 0%, 3%)	(235, 95%, 95%) (10%, 9%, 0%, 0%)
(235, 100%, 90%) (20%, 18%, 0%, 0%)	(235, 90%, 50%) (95%, 87%, 0%, 5%)	(235, 90%, 90%) (18%, 17%, 0%, 1%)
(235, 100%, 85%) (30%, 28%, 0%, 0%)	(235, 85%, 50%) (92%, 84%, 0%, 7%)	(235, 85%, 85%) (26%, 24%, 0%, 2%)
(235, 100%, 80%) (40%, 37%, 0%, 0%)	(235, 80%, 50%) (89%, 81%, 0%, 10%)	(235, 80%, 80%) (33%, 31%, 0%, 4%)
(235, 100%, 75%) (50%, 46%, 0%, 0%)	(235, 75%, 50%) (86%, 79%, 0%, 13%)	(235, 75%, 75%) (40%, 37%, 0%, 6%)
(235, 100%, 70%) (60%, 55%, 0%, 0%)	(235, 70%, 50%) (82%, 75%, 0%, 15%)	(235, 70%, 70%) (46%, 42%, 0%, 9%)
(235, 100%, 65%) (70%, 64%, 0%, 0%)	(235, 65%, 50%) (79%, 72%, 0%, 18%)	(235, 65%, 65%) (52%, 48%, 0%, 12%)
(235, 100%, 60%) (80%, 73%, 0%, 0%)	(235, 60%, 50%) (75%, 69%, 0%, 20%)	(235, 60%, 60%) (57%, 52%, 0%, 16%)
(235, 100%, 55%) (90%, 82%, 0%, 0%)	(235, 55%, 50%) (71%, 65%, 0%, 22%)	(235, 55%, 55%) (62%, 57%, 0%, 20%)
(235, 100%, 50%) (100%, 92%, 0%, 0%)	(235, 50%, 50%) (67%, 61%, 0%, 25%)	(235, 50%, 50%) (67%, 61%, 0%, 25%)
(235, 100%, 45%) (100%, 92%, 0%, 10%)	(235, 45%, 50%) (62%, 57%, 0%, 28%)	(235, 45%, 45%) (62%, 57%, 0%, 35%)
(235, 100%, 40%) (100%, 92%, 0%, 20%)	(235, 40%, 50%) (57%, 52%, 0%, 30%)	(235, 40, 40%) (57%, 52%, 0%, 44%)
(235, 100%, 35%) (100%, 92%, 0%, 30%)	(235, 35%, 50%) (52%, 48%, 0%, 32%)	(235, 35%, 35%) (52%, 48%, 0%, 53%)
(235, 100%, 30%) (100%, 92%, 0%, 40%)	(235, 30%, 50%) (46%, 42%, 0%, 35%)	(235, 30%, 30%) (46%, 42%, 0%, 61%)
(235, 100%, 25%) (100%, 92%, 0%, 50%)	(235, 25%, 50%) (40%, 37%, 0%, 38%)	(235, 25%, 25%) (40%, 37%, 0%, 69%)
(235, 100%, 20%) (100%, 92%, 0%, 60%)	(235, 20%, 50%) (33%, 31%, 0%, 40%)	(235, 20%, 20%) (33%, 31%, 0%, 76%)
(235, 100%, 15%) (100%, 92%, 0%, 70%)	(235, 15%, 50%) (26%, 24%, 0%, 43%)	(235, 15%, 15%) (26%, 24%, 0%, 83%)
(235, 100%, 10%) (100%, 92%, 0%, 80%)	(235, 10%, 50%) (18%, 17%, 0%, 45%)	(235, 10%, 10%) (18%, 17%, 0%, 89%)
(235, 100%, 5%) (100%, 92%, 0%, 90%)	(235, 5%, 50%) (10%, 9%, 0%, 47%)	(235, 5%, 5%) (10%, 9%, 0%, 95%)
(235, 100%, 0%) (0%, 0%, 0%, 100%)	(235, 0%, 50%) (0%, 0%, 0%, 50%)	(235, 0%, 0%) (0%, 0%, 0%, 100%)

H = 240, S = X%, L = X%	H = 240, S = X%, L = 50%	H = 240, S = 100%, L = X%
(240, 100%, 100%) (0%, 0%, 0%, 0%)	(240, 100%, 50%) (100%, 100%, 0%, 0%)	(240, 100%, 100%) (0%, 0%, 0%, 0%)
(240, 95%, 95%) (10%, 10%, 0%, 0%)	(240, 95%, 50%) (97%, 97%, 0%, 3%)	(240, 100%, 95%) (10%, 10%, 0%, 0%)
(240, 90%, 90%) (18%, 18%, 0%, 1%)	(240, 90%, 50%) (95%, 95%, 0%, 5%)	(240, 100%, 90%) (20%, 20%, 0%, 0%)
(240, 85%, 85%) (26%, 26%, 0%, 2%)	(240, 85%, 50%) (92%, 92%, 0%, 7%)	(240, 100%, 85%) (30%, 30%, 0%, 0%)
(240, 80%, 80%) (33%, 33%, 0%, 4%)	(240, 80%, 50%) (89%, 89%, 0%, 10%)	(240, 100%, 80%) (40%, 40%, 0%, 0%)
(240, 75%, 75%) (40%, 40%, 0%, 6%)	(240, 75%, 50%) (86%, 86%, 0%, 13%)	(240, 100%, 75%) (50%, 50%, 0%, 0%)
(240, 70%, 70%) (46%, 46%, 0%, 9%)	(240, 70%, 50%) (82%, 82%, 0%, 15%)	(240, 100%, 70%) (60%, 60%, 0%, 0%)
(240, 65%, 65%) (52%, 52%, 0%, 12%)	(240, 65%, 50%) (79%, 79%, 0%, 18%)	(240, 100%, 65%) (70%, 70%, 0%, 0%)
(240, 60%, 60%) (57%, 57%, 0%, 16%)	(240, 60%, 50%) (75%, 75%, 0%, 20%)	(240, 100%, 60%) (80%, 80%, 0%, 0%)
(240, 55%, 55%) (62%, 62%, 0%, 20%)	(240, 55%, 50%) (71%, 71%, 0%, 22%)	(240, 100%, 55%) (90%, 90%, 0%, 0%)
(240, 50%, 50%) (67%, 67%, 0%, 25%)	(240, 50%, 50%) (67%, 67%, 0%, 25%)	(240, 100%, 50%) (100%, 100%, 0%, 0%)
(240, 45%, 45%) (62%, 62%, 0%, 35%)	(240, 45%, 50%) (62%, 62%, 0%, 28%)	(240, 100%, 45%) (100%, 100%, 0%, 10%)
(240, 40, 40%) (57%, 57%, 0%, 44%)	(240, 40%, 50%) (57%, 57%, 0%, 30%)	(240, 100%, 40%) (100%, 100%, 0%, 20%)
(240, 35%, 35%) (52%, 52%, 0%, 53%)	(240, 35%, 50%) (52%, 52%, 0%, 32%)	(240, 100%, 35%) (100%, 100%, 0%, 30%)
(240, 30%, 30%) (46%, 46%, 0%, 61%)	(240, 30%, 50%) (46%, 46%, 0%, 35%)	(240, 100%, 30%) (100%, 100%, 0%, 40%)
(240, 25%, 25%) (40%, 40%, 0%, 69%)	(240, 25%, 50%) (40%, 40%, 0%, 38%)	(240, 100%, 25%) (100%, 100%, 0%, 50%)
(240, 20%, 20%) (33%, 33%, 0%, 76%)	(240, 20%, 50%) (33%, 33%, 0%, 40%)	(240, 100%, 20%) (100%, 100%, 0%, 60%)
(240, 15%, 15%) (26%, 26%, 0%, 83%)	(240, 15%, 50%) (26%, 26%, 0%, 43%)	(240, 100%, 15%) (100%, 100%, 0%, 70%)
(240, 10%, 10%) (18%, 18%, 0%, 89%)	(240, 10%, 50%) (18%, 18%, 0%, 45%)	(240, 100%, 10%) (100%, 100%, 0%, 80%)
(240, 5%, 5%) (10%, 10%, 0%, 95%)	(240, 5%, 50%) (10%, 10%, 0%, 47%)	(240, 100%, 5%) (100%, 100%, 0%, 90%)
(240, 0%, 0%) (0%, 0%, 0%, 100%)	(240, 0%, 50%) (0%, 0%, 0%, 50%)	(240, 100%, 0%) (0%, 0%, 0%, 100%)

H = 245, S = 100%, L = X%	H = 245, S = X%, L = 50%	H = 245, S = X%, L = X%
(245, 100%, 100%) (0%, 0%, 0%, 0%)	(245, 100%, 50%) (92%, 100%, 0%, 0%)	(245, 100%, 100%) (0%, 0%, 0%, 0%)
(245, 100%, 95%) (9%, 10%, 0%, 0%)	(245, 95%, 50%) (89%, 97%, 0%, 3%)	(245, 95%, 95%) (9%, 10%, 0%, 0%)
(245, 100%, 90%) (18%, 20%, 0%, 0%)	(245, 90%, 50%) (87%, 95%, 0%, 5%)	(245, 90%, 90%) (17%, 18%, 0%, 1%)
(245, 100%, 85%) (28%, 30%, 0%, 0%)	(245, 85%, 50%) (84%, 92%, 0%, 7%)	(245, 85%, 85%) (24%, 26%, 0%, 2%)
(245, 100%, 80%) (37%, 40%, 0%, 0%)	(245, 80%, 50%) (81%, 89%, 0%, 10%)	(245, 80%, 80%) (31%, 33%, 0%, 4%)
(245, 100%, 75%) (46%, 50%, 0%, 0%)	(245, 75%, 50%) (79%, 86%, 0%, 13%)	(245, 75%, 75%) (37%, 40%, 0%, 6%)
(245, 100%, 70%) (55%, 60%, 0%, 0%)	(245, 70%, 50%) (75%, 82%, 0%, 15%)	(245, 70%, 70%) (42%, 46%, 0%, 9%)
(245, 100%, 65%) (64%, 70%, 0%, 0%)	(245, 65%, 50%) (72%, 79%, 0%, 18%)	(245, 65%, 65%) (48%, 52%, 0%, 12%)
(245, 100%, 60%) (73%, 80%, 0%, 0%)	(245, 60%, 50%) (69%, 75%, 0%, 20%)	(245, 60%, 60%) (52%, 57%, 0%, 16%)
(245, 100%, 55%) (83%, 90%, 0%, 0%)	(245, 55%, 50%) (65%, 71%, 0%, 22%)	(245, 55%, 55%) (57%, 62%, 0%, 20%)
(245, 100%, 50%) (92%, 100%, 0%, 0%)	(245, 50%, 50%) (61%, 67%, 0%, 25%)	(245, 50%, 50%) (61%, 67%, 0%, 25%)
(245, 100%, 45%) (92%, 100%, 0%, 10%)	(245, 45%, 50%) (57%, 62%, 0%, 28%)	(245, 45%, 45%) (57%, 62%, 0%, 35%)
(245, 100%, 40%) (92%, 100%, 0%, 20%)	(245, 40%, 50%) (52%, 57%, 0%, 30%)	(245, 40, 40%) (52%, 57%, 0%, 44%)
(245, 100%, 35%) (92%, 100%, 0%, 30%)	(245, 35%, 50%) (48%, 52%, 0%, 32%)	(245, 35%, 35%) (48%, 52%, 0%, 53%)
(245, 100%, 30%) (92%, 100%, 0%, 40%)	(245, 30%, 50%) (42%, 46%, 0%, 35%)	(245, 30%, 30%) (42%, 46%, 0%, 61%)
(245, 100%, 25%) (92%, 100%, 0%, 50%)	(245, 25%, 50%) (37%, 40%, 0%, 38%)	(245, 25%, 25%) (37%, 40%, 0%, 69%)
(245, 100%, 20%) (92%, 100%, 0%, 60%)	(245, 20%, 50%) (31%, 33%, 0%, 40%)	(245, 20%, 20%) (31%, 33%, 0%, 76%)
(245, 100%, 15%) (92%, 100%, 0%, 70%)	(245, 15%, 50%) (24%, 26%, 0%, 43%)	(245, 15%, 15%) (24%, 26%, 0%, 83%)
(245, 100%, 10%) (92%, 100%, 0%, 80%)	(245, 10%, 50%) (17%, 18%, 0%, 45%)	(245, 10%, 10%) (17%, 18%, 0%, 89%)
(245, 100%, 5%) (92%, 100%, 0%, 90%)	(245, 5%, 50%) (9%, 10%, 0%, 47%)	(245, 5%, 5%) (9%, 10%, 0%, 95%)
(245, 100%, 0%) (0%, 0%, 0%, 100%)	(245, 0%, 50%) (0%, 0%, 0%, 50%)	(245, 0%, 0%) (0%, 0%, 0%, 100%)

H = 250, S = X%, L = X%	H = 250, S = X%, L = 50%	H = 250, S = 100%, L = X%
(250, 100%, 100%) (0%, 0%, 0%, 0%)	(250, 100%, 50%) (83%, 100%, 0%, 0%)	(250, 100%, 100%) (0%, 0%, 0%, 0%)
(250, 95%, 95%) (8%, 10%, 0%, 0%)	(250, 95%, 50%) (81%, 97%, 0%, 3%)	(250, 100%, 95%) (8%, 10%, 0%, 0%)
(250, 90%, 90%) (15%, 18%, 0%, 1%)	(250, 90%, 50%) (79%, 95%, 0%, 5%)	(250, 100%, 90%) (17%, 20%, 0%, 0%)
(250, 85%, 85%) (22%, 26%, 0%, 2%)	(250, 85%, 50%) (77%, 92%, 0%, 7%)	(250, 100%, 85%) (25%, 30%, 0%, 0%)
(250, 80%, 80%) (28%, 33%, 0%, 4%)	(250, 80%, 50%) (74%, 89%, 0%, 10%)	(250, 100%, 80%) (33%, 40%, 0%, 0%)
(250, 75%, 75%) (33%, 40%, 0%, 6%)	(250, 75%, 50%) (71%, 86%, 0%, 13%)	(250, 100%, 75%) (42%, 50%, 0%, 0%)
(250, 70%, 70%) (38%, 46%, 0%, 9%)	(250, 70%, 50%) (69%, 82%, 0%, 15%)	(250, 100%, 70%) (50%, 60%, 0%, 0%)
(250, 65%, 65%) (43%, 52%, 0%, 12%)	(250, 65%, 50%) (66%, 79%, 0%, 18%)	(250, 100%, 65%) (58%, 70%, 0%, 0%)
(250, 60%, 60%) (48%, 57%, 0%, 16%)	(250, 60%, 50%) (62%, 75%, 0%, 20%)	(250, 100%, 60%) (67%, 80%, 0%, 0%)
(250, 55%, 55%) (52%, 62%, 0%, 20%)	(250, 55%, 50%) (59%, 71%, 0%, 22%)	(250, 100%, 55%) (75%, 90%, 0%, 0%)
(250, 50%, 50%) (56%, 67%, 0%, 25%)	(250, 50%, 50%) (56%, 67%, 0%, 25%)	(250, 100%, 50%) (83%, 100%, 0%, 0%)
(250, 45%, 45%) (52%, 62%, 0%, 35%)	(250, 45%, 50%) (52%, 62%, 0%, 28%)	(250, 100%, 45%) (83%, 100%, 0%, 10%)
(250, 40, 40%) (48%, 57%, 0%, 44%)	(250, 40%, 50%) (48%, 57%, 0%, 30%)	(250, 100%, 40%) (83%, 100%, 0%, 20%)
(250, 35%, 35%) (43%, 52%, 0%, 53%)	(250, 35%, 50%) (43%, 52%, 0%, 32%)	(250, 100%, 35%) (83%, 100%, 0%, 30%)
(250, 30%, 30%) (38%, 46%, 0%, 61%)	(250, 30%, 50%) (38%, 46%, 0%, 35%)	(250, 100%, 30%) (83%, 100%, 0%, 40%)
(250, 25%, 25%) (33%, 40%, 0%, 69%)	(250, 25%, 50%) (33%, 40%, 0%, 38%)	(250, 100%, 25%) (83%, 100%, 0%, 50%)
(250, 20%, 20%) (28%, 33%, 0%, 76%)	(250, 20%, 50%) (28%, 33%, 0%, 40%)	(250, 100%, 20%) (83%, 100%, 0%, 60%)
(250, 15%, 15%) (22%, 26%, 0%, 83%)	(250, 15%, 50%) (22%, 26%, 0%, 43%)	(250, 100%, 15%) (83%, 100%, 0%, 70%)
(250, 10%, 10%) (15%, 18%, 0%, 89%)	(250, 10%, 50%) (15%, 18%, 0%, 45%)	(250, 100%, 10%) (83%, 100%, 0%, 80%)
(250, 5%, 5%) (8%, 10%, 0%, 95%)	(250, 5%, 50%) (8%, 10%, 0%, 47%)	(250, 100%, 5%) (83%, 100%, 0%, 90%)
(250, 0%, 0%) (0%, 0%, 0%, 100%)	(250, 0%, 50%) (0%, 0%, 0%, 50%)	(250, 100%, 0%) (0%, 0%, 0%, 100%)

H = 255, S = 100%, L = X%	H = 255, S = X%, L = 50%	H = 255, S = X%, L = X%
(255, 100%, 100%) (0%, 0%, 0%, 0%)	(255, 100%, 50%) (75%, 100%, 0%, 0%)	(255, 100%, 100%) (0%, 0%, 0%, 0%)
(255, 100%, 95%) (8%, 10%, 0%, 0%)	(255, 95%, 50%) (73%, 97%, 0%, 3%)	(255, 95%, 95%) (7%, 10%, 0%, 0%)
(255, 100%, 90%) (15%, 20%, 0%, 0%)	(255, 90%, 50%) (71%, 95%, 0%, 5%)	(255, 90%, 90%) (14%, 18%, 0%, 1%)
(255, 100%, 85%) (23%, 30%, 0%, 0%)	(255, 85%, 50%) (69%, 92%, 0%, 7%)	(255, 85%, 85%) (20%, 26%, 0%, 2%)
(255, 100%, 80%) (30%, 40%, 0%, 0%)	(255, 80%, 50%) (67%, 89%, 0%, 10%)	(255, 80%, 80%) (25%, 33%, 0%, 4%)
(255, 100%, 75%) (38%, 50%, 0%, 0%)	(255, 75%, 50%) (64%, 86%, 0%, 13%)	(255, 75%, 75%) (30%, 40%, 0%, 6%)
(255, 100%, 70%) (45%, 60%, 0%, 0%)	(255, 70%, 50%) (62%, 82%, 0%, 15%)	(255, 70%, 70%) (35%, 46%, 0%, 9%)
(255, 100%, 65%) (52%, 70%, 0%, 0%)	(255, 65%, 50%) (59%, 79%, 0%, 18%)	(255, 65%, 65%) (39%, 52%, 0%, 12%)
(255, 100%, 60%) (60%, 80%, 0%, 0%)	(255, 60%, 50%) (56%, 75%, 0%, 20%)	(255, 60%, 60%) (43%, 57%, 0%, 16%)
(255, 100%, 55%) (67%, 90%, 0%, 0%)	(255, 55%, 50%) (53%, 71%, 0%, 22%)	(255, 55%, 55%) (47%, 62%, 0%, 20%)
(255, 100%, 50%) (75%, 100%, 0%, 0%)	(255, 50%, 50%) (50%, 67%, 0%, 25%)	(255, 50%, 50%) (50%, 67%, 0%, 25%)
(255, 100%, 45%) (75%, 100%, 0%, 10%)	(255, 45%, 50%) (47%, 62%, 0%, 28%)	(255, 45%, 45%) (47%, 62%, 0%, 35%)
(255, 100%, 40%) (75%, 100%, 0%, 20%)	(255, 40%, 50%) (43%, 57%, 0%, 30%)	(255, 40, 40%) (43%, 57%, 0%, 44%)
(255, 100%, 35%) (75%, 100%, 0%, 30%)	(255, 35%, 50%) (39%, 52%, 0%, 32%)	(255, 35%, 35%) (39%, 52%, 0%, 53%)
(255, 100%, 30%) (75%, 100%, 0%, 40%)	(255, 30%, 50%) (35%, 46%, 0%, 35%)	(255, 30%, 30%) (35%, 46%, 0%, 61%)
(255, 100%, 25%) (75%, 100%, 0%, 50%)	(255, 25%, 50%) (30%, 40%, 0%, 38%)	(255, 25%, 25%) (30%, 40%, 0%, 69%)
(255, 100%, 20%) (75%, 100%, 0%, 60%)	(255, 20%, 50%) (25%, 33%, 0%, 40%)	(255, 20%, 20%) (25%, 33%, 0%, 76%)
(255, 100%, 15%) (75%, 100%, 0%, 70%)	(255, 15%, 50%) (20%, 26%, 0%, 43%)	(255, 15%, 15%) (20%, 26%, 0%, 83%)
(255, 100%, 10%) (75%, 100%, 0%, 80%)	(255, 10%, 50%) (14%, 18%, 0%, 45%)	(255, 10%, 10%) (14%, 18%, 0%, 89%)
(255, 100%, 5%) (75%, 100%, 0%, 90%)	(255, 5%, 50%) (7%, 10%, 0%, 47%)	(255, 5%, 5%) (7%, 10%, 0%, 95%)
(255, 100%, 0%) (0%, 0%, 0%, 100%)	(255, 0%, 50%) (0%, 0%, 0%, 50%)	(255, 0%, 0%) (0%, 0%, 0%, 100%)

H = 260, S = X%, L = X%	H = 260, S = X%, L = 50%	H = 260, S = 100%, L = X%
(260, 100%, 100%) (0%, 0%, 0%, 0%)	(260, 100%, 50%) (67%, 100%, 0%, 0%)	(260, 100%, 100%) (0%, 0%, 0%, 0%)
(260, 95%, 95%) (6%, 10%, 0%, 0%)	(260, 95%, 50%) (65%, 97%, 0%, 3%)	(260, 100%, 95%) (7%, 10%, 0%, 0%)
(260, 90%, 90%) (12%, 18%, 0%, 1%)	(260, 90%, 50%) (63%, 95%, 0%, 5%)	(260, 100%, 90%) (13%, 20%, 0%, 0%)
(260, 85%, 85%) (17%, 26%, 0%, 2%)	(260, 85%, 50%) (61%, 92%, 0%, 7%)	(260, 100%, 85%) (20%, 30%, 0%, 0%)
(260, 80%, 80%) (22%, 33%, 0%, 4%)	(260, 80%, 50%) (59%, 89%, 0%, 10%)	(260, 100%, 80%) (20%, 40%, 0%, 0%)
(260, 75%, 75%) (27%, 40%, 0%, 6%)	(260, 75%, 50%) (57%, 86%, 0%, 13%)	(260, 100%, 75%) (33%, 50%, 0%, 0%)
(260, 70%, 70%) (31%, 46%, 0%, 9%)	(260, 70%, 50%) (55%, 82%, 0%, 15%)	(260, 100%, 70%) (40%, 60%, 0%, 0%)
(260, 65%, 65%) (35%, 52%, 0%, 12%)	(260, 65%, 50%) (53%, 79%, 0%, 18%)	(260, 100%, 65%) (47%, 70%, 0%, 0%)
(260, 60%, 60%) (38%, 57%, 0%, 16%)	(260, 60%, 50%) (50%, 75%, 0%, 20%)	(260, 100%, 60%) (53%, 80%, 0%, 0%)
(260, 55%, 55%) (41%, 62%, 0%, 20%)	(260, 55%, 50%) (47%, 71%, 0%, 22%)	(260, 100%, 55%) (60%, 90%, 0%, 0%)
(260, 50%, 50%) (44%, 67%, 0%, 25%)	(260, 50%, 50%) (44%, 67%, 0%, 25%)	(260, 100%, 50%) (67%, 100%, 0%, 0%)
(260, 45%, 45%) (41%, 62%, 0%, 35%)	(260, 45%, 50%) (41%, 62%, 0%, 28%)	(260, 100%, 45%) (67%, 100%, 0%, 10%)
(260, 40, 40%) (38%, 57%, 0%, 44%)	(260, 40%, 50%) (38%, 57%, 0%, 30%)	(260, 100%, 40%) (67%, 100%, 0%, 20%)
(260, 35%, 35%) (35%, 52%, 0%, 53%)	(260, 35%, 50%) (35%, 52%, 0%, 32%)	(260, 100%, 35%) (67%, 100%, 0%, 30%)
(260, 30%, 30%) (31%, 46%, 0%, 61%)	(260, 30%, 50%) (31%, 46%, 0%, 35%)	(260, 100%, 30%) (67%, 100%, 0%, 40%)
(260, 25%, 25%) (27%, 40%, 0%, 69%)	(260, 25%, 50%) (27%, 40%, 0%, 38%)	(260, 100%, 25%) (67%, 100%, 0%, 50%)
(260, 20%, 20%) (22%, 33%, 0%, 76%)	(260, 20%, 50%) (22%, 33%, 0%, 40%)	(260, 100%, 20%) (67%, 100%, 0%, 60%)
(260, 15%, 15%) (17%, 26%, 0%, 83%)	(260, 15%, 50%) (17%, 26%, 0%, 43%)	(260, 100%, 15%) (67%, 100%, 0%, 70%)
(260, 10%, 10%) (12%, 18%, 0%, 89%)	(260, 10%, 50%) (12%, 18%, 0%, 45%)	(260, 100%, 10%) (67%, 100%, 0%, 80%)
(260, 5%, 5%) (6%, 10%, 0%, 95%)	(260, 5%, 50%) (6%, 10%, 0%, 47%)	(260, 100%, 5%) (67%, 100%, 0%, 90%)
(260, 0%, 0%) (0%, 0%, 0%, 100%)	(260, 0%, 50%) (0%, 0%, 0%, 50%)	(260, 100%, 0%) (0%, 0%, 0%, 100%)

H = 265, S = 100%, L = X%	H = 265, S = X%, L = 50%	H = 265, S = X%, L = X%
(265, 100%, 100%) (0%, 0%, 0%, 0%)	(265, 100%, 50%) (58%, 100%, 0%, 0%)	(265, 100%, 100%) (0%, 0%, 0%, 0%)
(265, 100%, 95%) (6%, 10%, 0%, 0%)	(265, 95%, 50%) (57%, 97%, 0%, 3%)	(265, 95%, 95%) (6%, 10%, 0%, 0%)
(265, 100%, 90%) (12%, 20%, 0%, 0%)	(265, 90%, 50%) (55%, 95%, 0%, 5%)	(265, 90%, 90%) (11%, 18%, 0%, 1%)
(265, 100%, 85%) (17%, 30%, 0%, 0%)	(265, 85%, 50%) (54%, 92%, 0%, 7%)	(265, 85%, 85%) (15%, 26%, 0%, 2%)
(265, 100%, 80%) (23%, 40%, 0%, 0%)	(265, 80%, 50%) (52%, 89%, 0%, 10%)	(265, 80%, 80%) (19%, 33%, 0%, 4%)
(265, 100%, 75%) (29%, 50%, 0%, 0%)	(265, 75%, 50%) (50%, 86%, 0%, 13%)	(265, 75%, 75%) (23%, 40%, 0%, 6%)
(265, 100%, 70%) (35%, 60%, 0%, 0%)	(265, 70%, 50%) (48%, 82%, 0%, 15%)	(265, 70%, 70%) (27%, 46%, 0%, 9%)
(265, 100%, 65%) (41%, 70%, 0%, 0%)	(265, 65%, 50%) (46%, 79%, 0%, 18%)	(265, 65%, 65%) (30%, 52%, 0%, 12%)
(265, 100%, 60%) (47%, 80%, 0%, 0%)	(265, 60%, 50%) (44%, 75%, 0%, 20%)	(265, 60%, 60%) (33%, 57%, 0%, 16%)
(265, 100%, 55%) (52%, 90%, 0%, 0%)	(265, 55%, 50%) (41%, 71%, 0%, 22%)	(265, 55%, 55%) (36%, 62%, 0%, 20%)
(265, 100%, 50%) (58%, 100%, 0%, 0%)	(265, 50%, 50%) (39%, 67%, 0%, 25%)	(265, 50%, 50%) (39%, 67%, 0%, 25%)
(265, 100%, 45%) (58%, 100%, 0%, 10%)	(265, 45%, 50%) (36%, 62%, 0%, 28%)	(265, 45%, 45%) (36%, 62%, 0%, 35%)
(265, 100%, 40%) (58%, 100%, 0%, 20%)	(265, 40%, 50%) (33%, 57%, 0%, 30%)	(265, 40, 40%) (33%, 57%, 0%, 44%)
(265, 100%, 35%) (58%, 100%, 0%, 30%)	(265, 35%, 50%) (30%, 52%, 0%, 32%)	(265, 35%, 35%) (30%, 52%, 0%, 53%)
(265, 100%, 30%) (58%, 100%, 0%, 40%)	(265, 30%, 50%) (27%, 46%, 0%, 35%)	(265, 30%, 30%) (27%, 46%, 0%, 61%)
(265, 100%, 25%) (58%, 100%, 0%, 50%)	(265, 25%, 50%) (23%, 40%, 0%, 38%)	(265, 25%, 25%) (23%, 40%, 0%, 69%)
(265, 100%, 20%) (58%, 100%, 0%, 60%)	(265, 20%, 50%) (19%, 33%, 0%, 40%)	(265, 20%, 20%) (19%, 33%, 0%, 76%)
(265, 100%, 15%) (58%, 100%, 0%, 70%)	(265, 15%, 50%) (15%, 26%, 0%, 43%)	(265, 15%, 15%) (15%, 26%, 0%, 83%)
(265, 100%, 10%) (58%, 100%, 0%, 80%)	(265, 10%, 50%) (11%, 18%, 0%, 45%)	(265, 10%, 10%) (11%, 18%, 0%, 89%)
(265, 100%, 5%) (58%, 100%, 0%, 90%)	(265, 5%, 50%) (6%, 10%, 0%, 47%)	(265, 5%, 5%) (6%, 10%, 0%, 95%)
(265, 100%, 0%) (0%, 0%, 0%, 100%)	(265, 0%, 50%) (0%, 0%, 0%, 50%)	(265, 0%, 0%) (0%, 0%, 0%, 100%)

H = 270, S = X%, L = X%	H = 270, S = X%, L = 50%	H = 270, S = 100%, L = X%
(270, 100%, 100%) (0%, 0%, 0%, 0%)	(270, 100%, 50%) (50%, 100%, 0%, 0%)	(270, 100%, 100%) (0%, 0%, 0%, 0%)
(270, 95%, 95%) (5%, 10%, 0%, 0%)	(270, 95%, 50%) (49%, 97%, 0%, 3%)	(270, 100%, 95%) (5%, 10%, 0%, 0%)
(270, 90%, 90%) (9%, 18%, 0%, 1%)	(270, 90%, 50%) (47%, 95%, 0%, 5%)	(270, 100%, 90%) (10%, 20%, 0%, 0%)
(270, 85%, 85%) (13%, 26%, 0%, 2%)	(270, 85%, 50%) (56%, 92%, 0%, 7%)	(270, 100%, 85%) (15%, 30%, 0%, 0%)
(270, 80%, 80%) (17%, 33%, 0%, 4%)	(270, 80%, 50%) (44%, 89%, 0%, 10%)	(270, 100%, 80%) (20%, 40%, 0%, 0%)
(270, 75%, 75%) (20%, 40%, 0%, 6%)	(270, 75%, 50%) (43%, 86%, 0%, 13%)	(270, 100%, 75%) (25%, 50%, 0%, 0%)
(270, 70%, 70%) (23%, 46%, 0%, 9%)	(270, 70%, 50%) (41%, 82%, 0%, 15%)	(270, 100%, 70%) (30%, 60%, 0%, 0%)
(270, 65%, 65%) (26%, 52%, 0%, 12%)	(270, 65%, 50%) (39%, 79%, 0%, 18%)	(270, 100%, 65%) (35%, 70%, 0%, 0%)
(270, 60%, 60%) (29%, 57%, 0%, 16%)	(270, 60%, 50%) (38%, 75%, 0%, 20%)	(270, 100%, 60%) (40%, 80%, 0%, 0%)
(270, 55%, 55%) (31%, 62%, 0%, 20%)	(270, 55%, 50%) (35%, 71%, 0%, 22%)	(270, 100%, 55%) (45%, 90%, 0%, 0%)
(270, 50%, 50%) (33%, 67%, 0%, 25%)	(270, 50%, 50%) (33%, 67%, 0%, 25%)	(270, 100%, 50%) (50%, 100%, 0%, 0%)
(270, 45%, 45%) (31%, 62%, 0%, 35%)	(270, 45%, 50%) (31%, 62%, 0%, 28%)	(270, 100%, 45%) (50%, 100%, 0%, 10%)
(270, 40, 40%) (29%, 57%, 0%, 44%)	(270, 40%, 50%) (29%, 57%, 0%, 30%)	(270, 100%, 40%) (50%, 100%, 0%, 20%)
(270, 35%, 35%) (26%, 52%, 0%, 53%)	(270, 35%, 50%) (26%, 52%, 0%, 32%)	(270, 100%, 35%) (50%, 100%, 0%, 30%)
(270, 30%, 30%) (23%, 46%, 0%, 61%)	(270, 30%, 50%) (23%, 46%, 0%, 35%)	(270, 100%, 30%) (50%, 100%, 0%, 40%)
(270, 25%, 25%) (20%, 40%, 0%, 69%)	(270, 25%, 50%) (20%, 40%, 0%, 38%)	(270, 100%, 25%) (50%, 100%, 0%, 50%)
(270, 20%, 20%) (17%, 33%, 0%, 76%)	(270, 20%, 50%) (17%, 33%, 0%, 40%)	(270, 100%, 20%) (50%, 100%, 0%, 60%)
(270, 15%, 15%) (13%, 26%, 0%, 83%)	(270, 15%, 50%) (13%, 26%, 0%, 43%)	(270, 100%, 15%) (50%, 100%, 0%, 70%)
(270, 10%, 10%) (9%, 18%, 0%, 89%)	(270, 10%, 50%) (9%, 18%, 0%, 45%)	(270, 100%, 10%) (50%, 100%, 0%, 80%)
(270, 5%, 5%) (5%, 10%, 0%, 95%)	(270, 5%, 50%) (5%, 10%, 0%, 47%)	(270, 100%, 5%) (50%, 100%, 0%, 90%)
(270, 0%, 0%) (0%, 0%, 0%, 100%)	(270, 0%, 50%) (0%, 0%, 0%, 50%)	(270, 100%, 0%) (0%, 0%, 0%, 100%)

H = 275, S = 100%, L = X%	H = 275, S = X%, L = 50%	H = 275, S = X%, L = X%
(275, 100%, 100%) (0%, 0%, 0%, 0%)	(275, 100%, 50%) (42%, 100%, 0%, 0%)	(275, 100%, 100%) (0%, 0%, 0%, 0%)
(275, 100%, 95%) (4%, 10%, 0%, 0%)	(275, 95%, 50%) (41%, 97%, 0%, 3%)	(275, 95%, 95%) (4%, 10%, 0%, 0%)
(275, 100%, 90%) (8%, 20%, 0%, 0%)	(275, 90%, 50%) (39%, 95%, 0%, 5%)	(275, 90%, 90%) (8%, 18%, 0%, 1%)
(275, 100%, 85%) (13%, 30%, 0%, 0%)	(275, 85%, 50%) (38%, 92%, 0%, 7%)	(275, 85%, 85%) (11%, 26%, 0%, 2%)
(275, 100%, 80%) (17%, 40%, 0%, 0%)	(275, 80%, 50%) (37%, 89%, 0%, 10%)	(275, 80%, 80%) (14%, 33%, 0%, 4%)
(275, 100%, 75%) (21%, 50%, 0%, 0%)	(275, 75%, 50%) (36%, 86%, 0%, 13%)	(275, 75%, 75%) (17%, 40%, 0%, 6%)
(275, 100%, 70%) (25%, 60%, 0%, 0%)	(275, 70%, 50%) (34%, 82%, 0%, 15%)	(275, 70%, 70%) (19%, 46%, 0%, 9%)
(275, 100%, 65%) (29%, 70%, 0%, 0%)	(275, 65%, 50%) (33%, 79%, 0%, 18%)	(275, 65%, 65%) (22%, 52%, 0%, 12%)
(275, 100%, 60%) (33%, 80%, 0%, 0%)	(275, 60%, 50%) (31%, 75%, 0%, 20%)	(275, 60%, 60%) (24%, 57%, 0%, 16%)
(275, 100%, 55%) (38%, 90%, 0%, 0%)	(275, 55%, 50%) (30%, 71%, 0%, 22%)	(275, 55%, 55%) (26%, 62%, 0%, 20%)
(275, 100%, 50%) (42%, 100%, 0%, 0%)	(275, 50%, 50%) (28%, 67%, 0%, 25%)	(275, 50%, 50%) (28%, 67%, 0%, 25%)
(275, 100%, 45%) (42%, 100%, 0%, 10%)	(275, 45%, 50%) (26%, 62%, 0%, 28%)	(275, 45%, 45%) (26%, 62%, 0%, 35%)
(275, 100%, 40%) (42%, 100%, 0%, 20%)	(275, 40%, 50%) (24%, 57%, 0%, 30%)	(275, 40, 40%) (24%, 57%, 0%, 44%)
(275, 100%, 35%) (42%, 100%, 0%, 30%)	(275, 35%, 50%) (22%, 52%, 0%, 32%)	(275, 35%, 35%) (22%, 52%, 0%, 53%)
(275, 100%, 30%) (42%, 100%, 0%, 40%)	(275, 30%, 50%) (19%, 46%, 0%, 35%)	(275, 30%, 30%) (19%, 46%, 0%, 61%)
(275, 100%, 25%) (42%, 100%, 0%, 50%)	(275, 25%, 50%) (17%, 40%, 0%, 38%)	(275, 25%, 25%) (17%, 40%, 0%, 69%)
(275, 100%, 20%) (42%, 100%, 0%, 60%)	(275, 20%, 50%) (14%, 33%, 0%, 40%)	(275, 20%, 20%) (14%, 33%, 0%, 76%)
(275, 100%, 15%) (42%, 100%, 0%, 70%)	(275, 15%, 50%) (11%, 26%, 0%, 43%)	(275, 15%, 15%) (11%, 26%, 0%, 83%)
(275, 100%, 10%) (42%, 100%, 0%, 80%)	(275, 10%, 50%) (8%, 18%, 0%, 45%)	(275, 10%, 10%) (8%, 18%, 0%, 89%)
(275, 100%, 5%) (42%, 100%, 0%, 90%)	(275, 5%, 50%) (4%, 10%, 0%, 47%)	(275, 5%, 5%) (4%, 10%, 0%, 95%)
(275, 100%, 0%) (0%, 0%, 0%, 100%)	(275, 0%, 50%) (0%, 0%, 0%, 50%)	(275, 0%, 0%) (0%, 0%, 0%, 100%)

H = 280, S = X%, L = X%	H = 280, S = X%, L = 50%	H = 280, S = 100%, L = X%
(280, 100%, 100%) (0%, 0%, 0%, 0%)	(280, 100%, 50%) (33%, 100%, 0%, 0%)	(280, 100%, 100%) (0%, 0%, 0%, 0%)
(280, 95%, 95%) (3%, 10%, 0%, 0%)	(280, 95%, 50%) (32%, 97%, 0%, 3%)	(280, 100%, 95%) (3%, 10%, 0%, 0%)
(280, 90%, 90%) (6%, 18%, 0%, 1%)	(280, 90%, 50%) (32%, 95%, 0%, 5%)	(280, 100%, 90%) (7%, 20%, 0%, 0%)
(280, 85%, 85%) (9%, 26%, 0%, 2%)	(280, 85%, 50%) (31%, 92%, 0%, 7%)	(280, 100%, 85%) (10%, 30%, 0%, 0%)
(280, 80%, 80%) (11%, 33%, 0%, 4%)	(280, 80%, 50%) (30%, 89%, 0%, 10%)	(280, 100%, 80%) (13%, 40%, 0%, 0%)
(280, 75%, 75%) (13%, 40%, 0%, 6%)	(280, 75%, 50%) (29%, 86%, 0%, 13%)	(280, 100%, 75%) (17%, 50%, 0%, 0%)
(280, 70%, 70%) (15%, 46%, 0%, 9%)	(280, 70%, 50%) (27%, 82%, 0%, 15%)	(280, 100%, 70%) (20%, 60%, 0%, 0%)
(280, 65%, 65%) (17%, 52%, 0%, 12%)	(280, 65%, 50%) (26%, 79%, 0%, 18%)	(280, 100%, 65%) (23%, 70%, 0%, 0%)
(280, 60%, 60%) (19%, 57%, 0%, 16%)	(280, 60%, 50%) (25%, 75%, 0%, 20%)	(280, 100%, 60%) (27%, 80%, 0%, 0%)
(280, 55%, 55%) (21%, 62%, 0%, 20%)	(280, 55%, 50%) (24%, 71%, 0%, 22%)	(280, 100%, 55%) (30%, 90%, 0%, 0%)
(280, 50%, 50%) (22%, 67%, 0%, 25%)	(280, 50%, 50%) (22%, 67%, 0%, 25%)	(280, 100%, 50%) (33%, 100%, 0%, 0%)
(280, 45%, 45%) (21%, 62%, 0%, 35%)	(280, 45%, 50%) (21%, 62%, 0%, 28%)	(280, 100%, 45%) (33%, 100%, 0%, 10%)
(280, 40, 40%) (19%, 57%, 0%, 44%)	(280, 40%, 50%) (19%, 57%, 0%, 30%)	(280, 100%, 40%) (33%, 100%, 0%, 20%)
(280, 35%, 35%) (17%, 52%, 0%, 53%)	(280, 35%, 50%) (17%, 52%, 0%, 32%)	(280, 100%, 35%) (33%, 100%, 0%, 30%)
(280, 30%, 30%) (15%, 46%, 0%, 61%)	(280, 30%, 50%) (15%, 46%, 0%, 35%)	(280, 100%, 30%) (33%, 100%, 0%, 40%)
(280, 25%, 25%) (13%, 40%, 0%, 69%)	(280, 25%, 50%) (13%, 40%, 0%, 38%)	(280, 100%, 25%) (33%, 100%, 0%, 50%)
(280, 20%, 20%) (11%, 33%, 0%, 76%)	(280, 20%, 50%) (11%, 33%, 0%, 40%)	(280, 100%, 20%) (33%, 100%, 0%, 60%)
(280, 15%, 15%) (9%, 26%, 0%, 83%)	(280, 15%, 50%) (9%, 26%, 0%, 43%)	(280, 100%, 15%) (33%, 100%, 0%, 70%)
(280, 10%, 10%) (6%, 18%, 0%, 89%)	(280, 10%, 50%) (6%, 18%, 0%, 45%)	(280, 100%, 10%) (33%, 100%, 0%, 80%)
(280, 5%, 5%) (3%, 10%, 0%, 95%)	(280, 5%, 50%) (3%, 10%, 0%, 47%)	(280, 100%, 5%) (33%, 100%, 0%, 90%)
(280, 0%, 0%) (0%, 0%, 0%, 100%)	(280, 0%, 50%) (0%, 0%, 0%, 50%)	(280, 100%, 0%) (0%, 0%, 0%, 100%)

H = 285, S = 100%, L = X%	H = 285, S = X%, L = 50%	H = 285, S = X%, L = X%
(285, 100%, 100%) (0%, 0%, 0%, 0%)	(285, 100%, 50%) (25%, 100%, 0%, 0%)	(285, 100%, 100%) (0%, 0%, 0%, 0%)
(285, 100%, 95%) (3%, 10%, 0%, 0%)	(285, 95%, 50%) (24%, 97%, 0%, 3%)	(285, 95%, 95%) (2%, 10%, 0%, 0%)
(285, 100%, 90%) (5%, 20%, 0%, 0%)	(285, 90%, 50%) (24%, 95%, 0%, 5%)	(285, 90%, 90%) (5%, 18%, 0%, 1%)
(285, 100%, 85%) (7%, 30%, 0%, 0%)	(285, 85%, 50%) (23%, 92%, 0%, 7%)	(285, 85%, 85%) (7%, 26%, 0%, 2%)
(285, 100%, 80%) (10%, 40%, 0%, 0%)	(285, 80%, 50%) (22%, 89%, 0%, 10%)	(285, 80%, 80%) (8%, 33%, 0%, 4%)
(285, 100%, 75%) (13%, 50%, 0%, 0%)	(285, 75%, 50%) (21%, 86%, 0%, 13%)	(285, 75%, 75%) (10%, 40%, 0%, 6%)
(285, 100%, 70%) (15%, 60%, 0%, 0%)	(285, 70%, 50%) (21%, 82%, 0%, 15%)	(285, 70%, 70%) (12%, 46%, 0%, 9%)
(285, 100%, 65%) (17%, 70%, 0%, 0%)	(285, 65%, 50%) (20%, 79%, 0%, 18%)	(285, 65%, 65%) (13%, 52%, 0%, 12%)
(285, 100%, 60%) (20%, 80%, 0%, 0%)	(285, 60%, 50%) (19%, 75%, 0%, 20%)	(285, 60%, 60%) (14%, 57%, 0%, 16%)
(285, 100%, 55%) (22%, 90%, 0%, 0%)	(285, 55%, 50%) (18%, 71%, 0%, 22%)	(285, 55%, 55%) (16%, 62%, 0%, 20%)
(285, 100%, 50%) (25%, 100%, 0%, 0%)	(285, 50%, 50%) (17%, 67%, 0%, 25%)	(285, 50%, 50%) (17%, 67%, 0%, 25%)
(285, 100%, 45%) (25%, 100%, 0%, 10%)	(285, 45%, 50%) (16%, 62%, 0%, 28%)	(285, 45%, 45%) (16%, 62%, 0%, 35%)
(285, 100%, 40%) (25%, 100%, 0%, 20%)	(285, 40%, 50%) (14%, 57%, 0%, 30%)	(285, 40, 40%) (14%, 57%, 0%, 44%)
(285, 100%, 35%) (25%, 100%, 0%, 30%)	(285, 35%, 50%) (13%, 52%, 0%, 32%)	(285, 35%, 35%) (13%, 52%, 0%, 53%)
(285, 100%, 30%) (25%, 100%, 0%, 40%)	(285, 30%, 50%) (12%, 46%, 0%, 35%)	(285, 30%, 30%) (12%, 46%, 0%, 61%)
(285, 100%, 25%) (25%, 100%, 0%, 50%)	(285, 25%, 50%) (10%, 40%, 0%, 38%)	(285, 25%, 25%) (10%, 40%, 0%, 69%)
(285, 100%, 20%) (25%, 100%, 0%, 60%)	(285, 20%, 50%) (8%, 33%, 0%, 40%)	(285, 20%, 20%) (8%, 33%, 0%, 76%)
(285, 100%, 15%) (25%, 100%, 0%, 70%)	(285, 15%, 50%) (7%, 26%, 0%, 43%)	(285, 15%, 15%) (7%, 26%, 0%, 83%)
(285, 100%, 10%) (25%, 100%, 0%, 80%)	(285, 10%, 50%) (5%, 18%, 0%, 45%)	(285, 10%, 10%) (5%, 18%, 0%, 89%)
(285, 100%, 5%) (25%, 100%, 0%, 90%)	(285, 5%, 50%) (2%, 10%, 0%, 47%)	(285, 5%, 5%) (2%, 10%, 0%, 95%)
(285, 100%, 0%) (0%, 0%, 0%, 100%)	(285, 0%, 50%) (0%, 0%, 0%, 50%)	(285, 0%, 0%) (0%, 0%, 0%, 100%)

H = 290, S = X%, L = X%	H = 290, S = X%, L = 50%	H = 290, S = 100%, L = X%
(290, 100%, 100%) (0%, 0%, 0%, 0%)	(290, 100%, 50%) (17%, 100%, 0%, 0%)	(290, 100%, 100%) (0%, 0%, 0%, 0%)
(290, 95%, 95%) (2%, 10%, 0%, 0%)	(290, 95%, 50%) (16%, 97%, 0%, 3%)	(290, 100%, 95%) (2%, 10%, 0%, 0%)
(290, 90%, 90%) (3%, 18%, 0%, 1%)	(290, 90%, 50%) (16%, 95%, 0%, 5%)	(290, 100%, 90%) (3%, 20%, 0%, 0%)
(290, 85%, 85%) (4%, 26%, 0%, 2%)	(290, 85%, 50%) (15%, 92%, 0%, 7%)	(290, 100%, 85%) (5%, 30%, 0%, 0%)
(290, 80%, 80%) (6%, 33%, 0%, 4%)	(290, 80%, 50%) (15%, 89%, 0%, 10%)	(290, 100%, 80%) (7%, 40%, 0%, 0%)
(290, 75%, 75%) (7%, 40%, 0%, 6%)	(290, 75%, 50%) (14%, 86%, 0%, 13%)	(290, 100%, 75%) (8%, 50%, 0%, 0%)
(290, 70%, 70%) (8%, 46%, 0%, 9%)	(290, 70%, 50%) (14%, 82%, 0%, 15%)	(290, 100%, 70%) (10%, 60%, 0%, 0%)
(290, 65%, 65%) (9%, 52%, 0%, 12%)	(290, 65%, 50%) (13%, 79%, 0%, 18%)	(290, 100%, 65%) (12%, 70%, 0%, 0%)
(290, 60%, 60%) (10%, 57%, 0%, 16%)	(290, 60%, 50%) (13%, 75%, 0%, 20%)	(290, 100%, 60%) (13%, 80%, 0%, 0%)
(290, 55%, 55%) (10%, 62%, 0%, 20%)	(290, 55%, 50%) (12%, 71%, 0%, 22%)	(290, 100%, 55%) (15%, 90%, 0%, 0%)
(290, 50%, 50%) (11%, 67%, 0%, 25%)	(290, 50%, 50%) (11%, 67%, 0%, 25%)	(290, 100%, 50%) (17%, 100%, 0%, 0%)
(290, 45%, 45%) (10%, 62%, 0%, 35%)	(290, 45%, 50%) (10%, 62%, 0%, 28%)	(290, 100%, 45%) (17%, 100%, 0%, 10%)
(290, 40, 40%) (10%, 57%, 0%, 44%)	(290, 40%, 50%) (10%, 57%, 0%, 30%)	(290, 100%, 40%) (17%, 100%, 0%, 20%)
(290, 35%, 35%) (9%, 52%, 0%, 53%)	(290, 35%, 50%) (9%, 52%, 0%, 32%)	(290, 100%, 35%) (17%, 100%, 0%, 30%)
(290, 30%, 30%) (8%, 46%, 0%, 61%)	(290, 30%, 50%) (8%, 46%, 0%, 35%)	(290, 100%, 30%) (17%, 100%, 0%, 40%)
(290, 25%, 25%) (7%, 40%, 0%, 69%)	(290, 25%, 50%) (7%, 40%, 0%, 38%)	(290, 100%, 25%) (17%, 100%, 0%, 50%)
(290, 20%, 20%) (6%, 33%, 0%, 76%)	(290, 20%, 50%) (6%, 33%, 0%, 40%)	(290, 100%, 20%) (17%, 100%, 0%, 60%)
(290, 15%, 15%) (4%, 26%, 0%, 83%)	(290, 15%, 50%) (4%, 26%, 0%, 43%)	(290, 100%, 15%) (17%, 100%, 0%, 70%)
(290, 10%, 10%) (3%, 18%, 0%, 89%)	(290, 10%, 50%) (3%, 18%, 0%, 45%)	(290, 100%, 10%) (17%, 100%, 0%, 80%)
(290, 5%, 5%) (2%, 10%, 0%, 95%)	(290, 5%, 50%) (2%, 10%, 0%, 47%)	(290, 100%, 5%) (17%, 100%, 0%, 90%)
(290, 0%, 0%) (0%, 0%, 0%, 100%)	(290, 0%, 50%) (0%, 0%, 0%, 50%)	(290, 100%, 0%) (0%, 0%, 0%, 100%)

H = 295, S = 100%, L = X%	H = 295, S = X%, L = 50%	H = 295, S = X%, L = X%
(295, 100%, 100%) (0%, 0%, 0%, 0%)	(295, 100%, 50%) (8%, 100%, 0%, 0%)	(295, 100%, 100%) (0%, 0%, 0%, 0%)
(295, 100%, 95%) (1%, 10%, 0%, 0%)	(295, 95%, 50%) (8%, 97%, 0%, 3%)	(295, 95%, 95%) (1%, 10%, 0%, 0%)
(295, 100%, 90%) (2%, 20%, 0%, 0%)	(295, 90%, 50%) (8%, 95%, 0%, 5%)	(295, 90%, 90%) (2%, 18%, 0%, 1%)
(295, 100%, 85%) (2%, 30%, 0%, 0%)	(295, 85%, 50%) (8%, 92%, 0%, 7%)	(295, 85%, 85%) (2%, 26%, 0%, 2%)
(295, 100%, 80%) (3%, 40%, 0%, 0%)	(295, 80%, 50%) (7%, 89%, 0%, 10%)	(295, 80%, 80%) (3%, 33%, 0%, 4%)
(295, 100%, 75%) (4%, 50%, 0%, 0%)	(295, 75%, 50%) (7%, 86%, 0%, 13%)	(295, 75%, 75%) (3%, 40%, 0%, 6%)
(295, 100%, 70%) (5%, 60%, 0%, 0%)	(295, 70%, 50%) (7%, 82%, 0%, 15%)	(295, 70%, 70%) (4%, 46%, 0%, 9%)
(295, 100%, 65%) (6%, 70%, 0%, 0%)	(295, 65%, 50%) (7%, 79%, 0%, 18%)	(295, 65%, 65%) (4%, 52%, 0%, 12%)
(295, 100%, 60%) (7%, 80%, 0%, 0%)	(295, 60%, 50%) (6%, 75%, 0%, 20%)	(295, 60%, 60%) (5%, 57%, 0%, 16%)
(295, 100%, 55%) (7%, 90%, 0%, 0%)	(295, 55%, 50%) (6%, 71%, 0%, 22%)	(295, 55%, 55%) (5%, 62%, 0%, 20%)
(295, 100%, 50%) (8%, 100%, 0%, 0%)	(295, 50%, 50%) (6%, 67%, 0%, 25%)	(295, 50%, 50%) (6%, 67%, 0%, 25%)
(295, 100%, 45%) (8%, 100%, 0%, 10%)	(295, 45%, 50%) (5%, 62%, 0%, 28%)	(295, 45%, 45%) (5%, 62%, 0%, 35%)
(295, 100%, 40%) (8%, 100%, 0%, 20%)	(295, 40%, 50%) (5%, 57%, 0%, 30%)	(295, 40, 40%) (5%, 57%, 0%, 44%)
(295, 100%, 35%) (8%, 100%, 0%, 30%)	(295, 35%, 50%) (4%, 52%, 0%, 32%)	(295, 35%, 35%) (4%, 52%, 0%, 53%)
(295, 100%, 30%) (8%, 100%, 0%, 40%)	(295, 30%, 50%) (4%, 46%, 0%, 35%)	(295, 30%, 30%) (4%, 46%, 0%, 61%)
(295, 100%, 25%) (8%, 100%, 0%, 50%)	(295, 25%, 50%) (3%, 40%, 0%, 38%)	(295, 25%, 25%) (3%, 40%, 0%, 69%)
(295, 100%, 20%) (8%, 100%, 0%, 60%)	(295, 20%, 50%) (3%, 33%, 0%, 40%)	(295, 20%, 20%) (3%, 33%, 0%, 76%)
(295, 100%, 15%) (8%, 100%, 0%, 70%)	(295, 15%, 50%) (2%, 26%, 0%, 43%)	(295, 15%, 15%) (2%, 26%, 0%, 83%)
(295, 100%, 10%) (8%, 100%, 0%, 80%)	(295, 10%, 50%) (2%, 18%, 0%, 45%)	(295, 10%, 10%) (2%, 18%, 0%, 89%)
(295, 100%, 5%) (8%, 100%, 0%, 90%)	(295, 5%, 50%) (1%, 10%, 0%, 47%)	(295, 5%, 5%) (1%, 10%, 0%, 95%)
(295, 100%, 0%) (0%, 0%, 0%, 100%)	(295, 0%, 50%) (0%, 0%, 0%, 50%)	(295, 0%, 0%) (0%, 0%, 0%, 100%)

H = 300, S = X%, L = X%	H = 300, S = X%, L = 50%	H = 300, S = 100%, L = X%
(300, 100%, 100%) (0%, 0%, 0%, 0%)	(300, 100%, 50%) (0%, 100%, 0%, 0%)	(300, 100%, 100%) (0%, 0%, 0%, 0%)
(300, 95%, 95%) (0%, 10%, 0%, 0%)	(300, 95%, 50%) (0%, 97%, 0%, 3%)	(300, 100%, 95%) (0%, 10%, 0%, 0%)
(300, 90%, 90%) (0%, 18%, 0%, 1%)	(300, 90%, 50%) (0%, 95%, 0%, 5%)	(300, 100%, 90%) (0%, 20%, 0%, 0%)
(300, 85%, 85%) (0%, 26%, 0%, 2%)	(300, 85%, 50%) (0%, 92%, 0%, 7%)	(300, 100%, 85%) (0%, 30%, 0%, 0%)
(300, 80%, 80%) (0%, 33%, 0%, 4%)	(300, 80%, 50%) (0%, 89%, 0%, 10%)	(300, 100%, 80%) (0%, 40%, 0%, 0%)
(300, 75%, 75%) (0%, 40%, 0%, 6%)	(300, 75%, 50%) (0%, 86%, 0%, 13%)	(300, 100%, 75%) (0%, 50%, 0%, 0%)
(300, 70%, 70%) (0%, 46%, 0%, 9%)	(300, 70%, 50%) (0%, 82%, 0%, 15%)	(300, 100%, 70%) (0%, 60%, 0%, 0%)
(300, 65%, 65%) (0%, 52%, 0%, 12%)	(300, 65%, 50%) (0%, 79%, 0%, 18%)	(300, 100%, 65%) (0%, 70%, 0%, 0%)
(300, 60%, 60%) (0%, 57%, 0%, 16%)	(300, 60%, 50%) (0%, 75%, 0%, 20%)	(300, 100%, 60%) (0%, 80%, 0%, 0%)
(300, 55%, 55%) (0%, 62%, 0%, 20%)	(300, 55%, 50%) (0%, 71%, 0%, 22%)	(300, 100%, 55%) (0%, 90%, 0%, 0%)
(300, 50%, 50%) (0%, 67%, 0%, 25%)	(300, 50%, 50%) (0%, 67%, 0%, 25%)	(300, 100%, 50%) (0%, 100%, 0%, 0%)
(300, 45%, 45%) (0%, 62%, 0%, 35%)	(300, 45%, 50%) (0%, 62%, 0%, 28%)	(300, 100%, 45%) (0%, 100%, 0%, 10%)
(300, 40, 40%) (0%, 57%, 0%, 44%)	(300, 40%, 50%) (0%, 57%, 0%, 30%)	(300, 100%, 40%) (0%, 100%, 0%, 20%)
(300, 35%, 35%) (0%, 52%, 0%, 53%)	(300, 35%, 50%) (0%, 52%, 0%, 32%)	(300, 100%, 35%) (0%, 100%, 0%, 30%)
(300, 30%, 30%) (0%, 46%, 0%, 61%)	(300, 30%, 50%) (0%, 46%, 0%, 35%)	(300, 100%, 30%) (0%, 100%, 0%, 40%)
(300, 25%, 25%) (0%, 40%, 0%, 69%)	(300, 25%, 50%) (0%, 40%, 0%, 38%)	(300, 100%, 25%) (0%, 100%, 0%, 50%)
(300, 20%, 20%) (0%, 33%, 0%, 76%)	(300, 20%, 50%) (0%, 33%, 0%, 40%)	(300, 100%, 20%) (0%, 100%, 0%, 60%)
(300, 15%, 15%) (0%, 26%, 0%, 83%)	(300, 15%, 50%) (0%, 26%, 0%, 43%)	(300, 100%, 15%) (0%, 100%, 0%, 70%)
(300, 10%, 10%) (0%, 18%, 0%, 89%)	(300, 10%, 50%) (0%, 18%, 0%, 45%)	(300, 100%, 10%) (0%, 100%, 0%, 80%)
(300, 5%, 5%) (0%, 10%, 0%, 95%)	(300, 5%, 50%) (0%, 10%, 0%, 47%)	(300, 100%, 5%) (0%, 100%, 0%, 90%)
(300, 0%, 0%) (0%, 0%, 0%, 100%)	(300, 0%, 50%) (0%, 0%, 0%, 50%)	(300, 100%, 0%) (0%, 0%, 0%, 100%)

H = 305, S = 100%, L = X%	H = 305, S = X%, L = 50%	H = 305, S = X%, L = X%
(305, 100%, 100%) (0%, 0%, 0%, 0%)	(305, 100%, 50%) (0%, 100%, 8%, 0%)	(305, 100%, 100%) (0%, 0%, 0%, 0%)
(305, 100%, 95%) (0%, 10%, 1%, 0%)	(305, 95%, 50%) (0%, 97%, 8%, 3%)	(305, 95%, 95%) (0%, 10%, 1%, 0%)
(305, 100%, 90%) (0%, 20%, 2%, 0%)	(305, 90%, 50%) (0%, 95%, 8%, 5%)	(305, 90%, 90%) (0%, 18%, 2%, 1%)
(305, 100%, 85%) (0%, 30%, 2%, 0%)	(305, 85%, 50%) (0%, 92%, 8%, 7%)	(305, 85%, 85%) (0%, 26%, 2%, 2%)
(305, 100%, 80%) (0%, 40%, 3%, 0%)	(305, 80%, 50%) (0%, 89%, 7%, 10%)	(305, 80%, 80%) (0%, 33%, 3%, 4%)
(305, 100%, 75%) (0%, 50%, 4%, 0%)	(305, 75%, 50%) (0%, 86%, 7%, 13%)	(305, 75%, 75%) (0%, 40%, 3%, 6%)
(305, 100%, 70%) (0%, 60%, 5%, 0%)	(305, 70%, 50%) (0%, 82%, 7%, 15%)	(305, 70%, 70%) (0%, 46%, 4%, 9%)
(305, 100%, 65%) (0%, 70%, 6%, 0%)	(305, 65%, 50%) (0%, 79%, 7%, 18%)	(305, 65%, 65%) (0%, 52%, 4%, 12%)
(305, 100%, 60%) (0%, 80%, 7%, 0%)	(305, 60%, 50%) (0%, 75%, 6%, 20%)	(305, 60%, 60%) (0%, 57%, 5%, 16%)
(305, 100%, 55%) (0%, 90%, 7%, 0%)	(305, 55%, 50%) (0%, 71%, 6%, 22%)	(305, 55%, 55%) (0%, 62%, 5%, 20%)
(305, 100%, 50%) (0%, 100%, 8%, 0%)	(305, 50%, 50%) (0%, 67%, 6%, 25%)	(305, 50%, 50%) (0%, 67%, 6%, 25%)
(305, 100%, 45%) (0%, 100%, 8%, 10%)	(305, 45%, 50%) (0%, 62%, 5%, 28%)	(305, 45%, 45%) (0%, 62%, 5%, 35%)
(305, 100%, 40%) (0%, 100%, 8%, 20%)	(305, 40%, 50%) (0%, 57%, 5%, 30%)	(305, 40, 40%) (0%, 57%, 5%, 44%)
(305, 100%, 35%) (0%, 100%, 8%, 30%)	(305, 35%, 50%) (0%, 52%, 4%, 32%)	(305, 35%, 35%) (0%, 52%, 4%, 53%)
(305, 100%, 30%) (0%, 100%, 8%, 40%)	(305, 30%, 50%) (0%, 46%, 4%, 35%)	(305, 30%, 30%) (0%, 46%, 4%, 61%)
(305, 100%, 25%) (0%, 100%, 8%, 50%)	(305, 25%, 50%) (0%, 40%, 3%, 38%)	(305, 25%, 25%) (0%, 40%, 3%, 69%)
(305, 100%, 20%) (0%, 100%, 8%, 60%)	(305, 20%, 50%) (0%, 33%, 3%, 40%)	(305, 20%, 20%) (0%, 33%, 3%, 76%)
(305, 100%, 15%) (0%, 100%, 8%, 70%)	(305, 15%, 50%) (0%, 26%, 2%, 43%)	(305, 15%, 15%) (0%, 26%, 2%, 83%)
(305, 100%, 10%) (0%, 100%, 8%, 80%)	(305, 10%, 50%) (0%, 18%, 2%, 45%)	(305, 10%, 10%) (0%, 18%, 2%, 89%)
(305, 100%, 5%) (0%, 100%, 8%, 90%)	(305, 5%, 50%) (0%, 10%, 1%, 47%)	(305, 5%, 5%) (0%, 10%, 1%, 95%)
(305, 100%, 0%) (0%, 0%, 0%, 100%)	(305, 0%, 50%) (0%, 0%, 0%, 50%)	(305, 0%, 0%) (0%, 0%, 0%, 100%)

H = 310, S = X%, L = X%	H = 310, S = X%, L = 50%	H = 310, S = 100%, L = X%
(310, 100%, 100%) (0%, 0%, 0%, 0%)	(310, 100%, 50%) (0%, 100%, 17%, 0%)	(310, 100%, 100%) (0%, 0%, 0%, 0%)
(310, 95%, 95%) (0%, 10%, 2%, 0%)	(310, 95%, 50%) (0%, 97%, 16%, 3%)	(310, 100%, 95%) (0%, 10%, 2%, 0%)
(310, 90%, 90%) (0%, 18%, 3%, 1%)	(310, 90%, 50%) (0%, 95%, 16%, 5%)	(310, 100%, 90%) (0%, 20%, 3%, 0%)
(310, 85%, 85%) (0%, 26%, 4%, 2%)	(310, 85%, 50%) (0%, 92%, 15%, 7%)	(310, 100%, 85%) (0%, 30%, 5%, 0%)
(310, 80%, 80%) (0%, 33%, 6%, 4%)	(310, 80%, 50%) (0%, 89%, 15%, 10%)	(310, 100%, 80%) (0%, 40%, 7%, 0%)
(310, 75%, 75%) (0%, 40%, 7%, 6%)	(310, 75%, 50%) (0%, 86%, 14%, 13%)	(310, 100%, 75%) (0%, 50%, 8%, 0%)
(310, 70%, 70%) (0%, 46%, 8%, 9%)	(310, 70%, 50%) (0%, 82%, 14%, 15%)	(310, 100%, 70%) (0%, 60%, 10%, 0%)
(310, 65%, 65%) (0%, 52%, 9%, 12%)	(310, 65%, 50%) (0%, 79%, 13%, 18%)	(310, 100%, 65%) (0%, 70%, 12%, 0%)
(310, 60%, 60%) (0%, 57%, 10%, 16%)	(310, 60%, 50%) (0%, 75%, 13%, 20%)	(310, 100%, 60%) (0%, 80%, 13%, 0%)
(310, 55%, 55%) (0%, 62%, 10%, 20%)	(310, 55%, 50%) (0%, 71%, 12%, 22%)	(310, 100%, 55%) (0%, 90%, 15%, 0%)
(310, 50%, 50%) (0%, 67%, 11%, 25%)	(310, 50%, 50%) (0%, 67%, 11%, 25%)	(310, 100%, 50%) (0%, 100%, 17%, 0%)
(310, 45%, 45%) (0%, 62%, 10%, 35%)	(310, 45%, 50%) (0%, 62%, 10%, 28%)	(310, 100%, 45%) (0%, 100%, 17%, 10%)
(310, 40, 40%) (0%, 57%, 10%, 44%)	(310, 40%, 50%) (0%, 57%, 10%, 30%)	(310, 100%, 40%) (0%, 100%, 17%, 20%)
(310, 35%, 35%) (0%, 52%, 9%, 53%)	(310, 35%, 50%) (0%, 52%, 9%, 32%)	(310, 100%, 35%) (0%, 100%, 17%, 30%)
(310, 30%, 30%) (0%, 46%, 8%, 61%)	(310, 30%, 50%) (0%, 46%, 8%, 35%)	(310, 100%, 30%) (0%, 100%, 17%, 40%)
(310, 25%, 25%) (0%, 40%, 7%, 69%)	(310, 25%, 50%) (0%, 40%, 7%, 38%)	(310, 100%, 25%) (0%, 100%, 17%, 50%)
(310, 20%, 20%) (0%, 33%, 6%, 76%)	(310, 20%, 50%) (0%, 33%, 6%, 40%)	(310, 100%, 20%) (0%, 100%, 17%, 60%)
(310, 15%, 15%) (0%, 26%, 4%, 83%)	(310, 15%, 50%) (0%, 26%, 4%, 43%)	(310, 100%, 15%) (0%, 100%, 17%, 70%)
(310, 10%, 10%) (0%, 18%, 3%, 89%)	(310, 10%, 50%) (0%, 18%, 3%, 45%)	(310, 100%, 10%) (0%, 100%, 17%, 80%)
(310, 5%, 5%) (0%, 10%, 2%, 95%)	(310, 5%, 50%) (0%, 10%, 2%, 47%)	(310, 100%, 5%) (0%, 100%, 17%, 90%)
(310, 0%, 0%) (0%, 0%, 0%, 100%)	(310, 0%, 50%) (0%, 0%, 0%, 50%)	(310, 100%, 0%) (0%, 0%, 0%, 100%)

H = 315, S = 100%, L = X%	H = 315, S = X%, L = 50%	H = 315, S = X%, L = X%
(315, 100%, 100%) (0%, 0%, 0%, 0%)	(315, 100%, 50%) (0%, 100%, 25%, 0%)	(315, 100%, 100%) (0%, 0%, 0%, 0%)
(315, 100%, 95%) (0%, 10%, 3%, 0%)	(315, 95%, 50%) (0%, 97%, 24%, 3%)	(315, 95%, 95%) (0%, 10%, 2%, 0%)
(315, 100%, 90%) (0%, 20%, 5%, 0%)	(315, 90%, 50%) (0%, 95%, 24%, 5%)	(315, 90%, 90%) (0%, 18%, 5%, 1%)
(315, 100%, 85%) (0%, 30%, 7%, 0%)	(315, 85%, 50%) (0%, 92%, 23%, 7%)	(315, 85%, 85%) (0%, 26%, 7%, 2%)
(315, 100%, 80%) (0%, 40%, 10%, 0%)	(315, 80%, 50%) (0%, 89%, 22%, 10%)	(315, 80%, 80%) (0%, 33%, 8%, 4%)
(315, 100%, 75%) (0%, 50%, 13%, 0%)	(315, 75%, 50%) (0%, 86%, 21%, 13%)	(315, 75%, 75%) (0%, 40%, 10%, 6%)
(315, 100%, 70%) (0%, 60%, 15%, 0%)	(315, 70%, 50%) (0%, 82%, 21%, 15%)	(315, 70%, 70%) (0%, 46%, 12%, 9%)
(315, 100%, 65%) (0%, 70%, 17%, 0%)	(315, 65%, 50%) (0%, 79%, 20%, 18%)	(315, 65%, 65%) (0%, 52%, 13%, 12%)
(315, 100%, 60%) (0%, 80%, 20%, 0%)	(315, 60%, 50%) (0%, 75%, 19%, 20%)	(315, 60%, 60%) (0%, 57%, 14%, 16%)
(315, 100%, 55%) (0%, 90%, 22%, 0%)	(315, 55%, 50%) (0%, 71%, 18%, 22%)	(315, 55%, 55%) (0%, 62%, 16%, 20%)
(315, 100%, 50%) (0%, 100%, 25%, 0%)	(315, 50%, 50%) (0%, 67%, 17%, 25%)	(315, 50%, 50%) (0%, 67%, 17%, 25%)
(315, 100%, 45%) (0%, 100%, 25%, 10%)	(315, 45%, 50%) (0%, 62%, 16%, 28%)	(315, 45%, 45%) (0%, 62%, 16%, 35%)
(315, 100%, 40%) (0%, 100%, 25%, 20%)	(315, 40%, 50%) (0%, 57%, 14%, 30%)	(315, 40, 40%) (0%, 57%, 14%, 44%)
(315, 100%, 35%) (0%, 100%, 25%, 30%)	(315, 35%, 50%) (0%, 52%, 13%, 32%)	(315, 35%, 35%) (0%, 52%, 13%, 53%)
(315, 100%, 30%) (0%, 100%, 25%, 40%)	(315, 30%, 50%) (0%, 46%, 12%, 35%)	(315, 30%, 30%) (0%, 46%, 12%, 61%)
(315, 100%, 25%) (0%, 100%, 25%, 50%)	(315, 25%, 50%) (0%, 40%, 10%, 38%)	(315, 25%, 25%) (0%, 40%, 10%, 69%)
(315, 100%, 20%) (0%, 100%, 25%, 60%)	(315, 20%, 50%) (0%, 33%, 8%, 40%)	(315, 20%, 20%) (0%, 33%, 8%, 76%)
(315, 100%, 15%) (0%, 100%, 25%, 70%)	(315, 15%, 50%) (0%, 26%, 7%, 43%)	(315, 15%, 15%) (0%, 26%, 7%, 83%)
(315, 100%, 10%) (0%, 100%, 25%, 80%)	(315, 10%, 50%) (0%, 18%, 5%, 45%)	(315, 10%, 10%) (0%, 18%, 5%, 89%)
(315, 100%, 5%) (0%, 100%, 25%, 90%)	(315, 5%, 50%) (0%, 10%, 2%, 47%)	(315, 5%, 5%) (0%, 10%, 2%, 95%)
(315, 100%, 0%) (0%, 0%, 0%, 100%)	(315, 0%, 50%) (0%, 0%, 0%, 50%)	(315, 0%, 0%) (0%, 0%, 0%, 100%)

H = 320, S = X%, L = X%	H = 320, S = X%, L = 50%	H = 320, S = 100%, L = X%
(320, 100%, 100%) (0%, 0%, 0%, 0%)	(320, 100%, 50%) (0%, 100%, 33%, 0%)	(320, 100%, 100%) (0%, 0%, 0%, 0%)
(320, 95%, 95%) (0%, 10%, 3%, 0%)	(320, 95%, 50%) (0%, 97%, 32%, 3%)	(320, 100%, 95%) (0%, 10%, 3%, 0%)
(320, 90%, 90%) (0%, 18%, 6%, 1%)	(320, 90%, 50%) (0%, 95%, 32%, 5%)	(320, 100%, 90%) (0%, 20%, 7%, 0%)
(320, 85%, 85%) (0%, 26%, 9%, 2%)	(320, 85%, 50%) (0%, 92%, 31%, 7%)	(320, 100%, 85%) (0%, 30%, 10%, 0%)
(320, 80%, 80%) (0%, 33%, 11%, 4%)	(320, 80%, 50%) (0%, 89%, 30%, 10%)	(320, 100%, 80%) (0%, 40%, 13%, 0%)
(320, 75%, 75%) (0%, 40%, 13%, 6%)	(320, 75%, 50%) (0%, 86%, 29%, 13%)	(320, 100%, 75%) (0%, 50%, 17%, 0%)
(320, 70%, 70%) (0%, 46%, 15%, 9%)	(320, 70%, 50%) (0%, 82%, 27%, 15%)	(320, 100%, 70%) (0%, 60%, 20%, 0%)
(320, 65%, 65%) (0%, 52%, 17%, 12%)	(320, 65%, 50%) (0%, 79%, 26%, 18%)	(320, 100%, 65%) (0%, 70%, 23%, 0%)
(320, 60%, 60%) (0%, 57%, 19%, 16%)	(320, 60%, 50%) (0%, 75%, 25%, 20%)	(320, 100%, 60%) (0%, 80%, 27%, 0%)
(320, 55%, 55%) (0%, 62%, 21%, 20%)	(320, 55%, 50%) (0%, 71%, 24%, 22%)	(320, 100%, 55%) (0%, 90%, 30%, 0%)
(320, 50%, 50%) (0%, 67%, 22%, 25%)	(320, 50%, 50%) (0%, 67%, 22%, 25%)	(320, 100%, 50%) (0%, 100%, 33%, 0%)
(320, 45%, 45%) (0%, 62%, 21%, 35%)	(320, 45%, 50%) (0%, 62%, 21%, 28%)	(320, 100%, 45%) (0%, 100%, 33%, 10%)
(320, 40, 40%) (0%, 57%, 19%, 44%)	(320, 40%, 50%) (0%, 57%, 19%, 30%)	(320, 100%, 40%) (0%, 100%, 33%, 20%)
(320, 35%, 35%) (0%, 52%, 17%, 53%)	(320, 35%, 50%) (0%, 52%, 17%, 32%)	(320, 100%, 35%) (0%, 100%, 33%, 30%)
(320, 30%, 30%) (0%, 46%, 15%, 61%)	(320, 30%, 50%) (0%, 46%, 15%, 35%)	(320, 100%, 30%) (0%, 100%, 33%, 40%)
(320, 25%, 25%) (0%, 40%, 13%, 69%)	(320, 25%, 50%) (0%, 40%, 13%, 38%)	(320, 100%, 25%) (0%, 100%, 33%, 50%)
(320, 20%, 20%) (0%, 33%, 11%, 76%)	(320, 20%, 50%) (0%, 33%, 11%, 40%)	(320, 100%, 20%) (0%, 100%, 33%, 60%)
(320, 15%, 15%) (0%, 26%, 9%, 83%)	(320, 15%, 50%) (0%, 26%, 9%, 43%)	(320, 100%, 15%) (0%, 100%, 33%, 70%)
(320, 10%, 10%) (0%, 18%, 6%, 89%)	(320, 10%, 50%) (0%, 18%, 6%, 45%)	(320, 100%, 10%) (0%, 100%, 33%, 80%)
(320, 5%, 5%) (0%, 10%, 3%, 95%)	(320, 5%, 50%) (0%, 10%, 3%, 47%)	(320, 100%, 5%) (0%, 100%, 33%, 90%)
(320, 0%, 0%) (0%, 0%, 0%, 100%)	(320, 0%, 50%) (0%, 0%, 0%, 50%)	(320, 100%, 0%) (0%, 0%, 0%, 100%)

H = 325, S = 100%, L = X%	H = 325, S = X%, L = 50%	H = 325, S = X%, L = X%
(325, 100%, 100%) (0%, 0%, 0%, 0%)	(325, 100%, 50%) (0%, 100%, 42%, 0%)	(325, 100%, 100%) (0%, 0%, 0%, 0%)
(325, 100%, 95%) (0%, 10%, 4%, 0%)	(325, 95%, 50%) (0%, 97%, 41%, 3%)	(325, 95%, 95%) (0%, 10%, 4%, 0%)
(325, 100%, 90%) (0%, 20%, 8%, 0%)	(325, 90%, 50%) (0%, 95%, 39%, 5%)	(325, 90%, 90%) (0%, 18%, 8%, 1%)
(325, 100%, 85%) (0%, 30%, 13%, 0%)	(325, 85%, 50%) (0%, 92%, 38%, 7%)	(325, 85%, 85%) (0%, 26%, 11%, 2%)
(325, 100%, 80%) (0%, 40%, 17%, 0%)	(325, 80%, 50%) (0%, 89%, 37%, 10%)	(325, 80%, 80%) (0%, 33%, 14%, 4%)
(325, 100%, 75%) (0%, 50%, 21%, 0%)	(325, 75%, 50%) (0%, 86%, 36%, 13%)	(325, 75%, 75%) (0%, 40%, 17%, 6%)
(325, 100%, 70%) (0%, 60%, 25%, 0%)	(325, 70%, 50%) (0%, 82%, 34%, 15%)	(325, 70%, 70%) (0%, 46%, 19%, 9%)
(325, 100%, 65%) (0%, 70%, 29%, 0%)	(325, 65%, 50%) (0%, 79%, 33%, 18%)	(325, 65%, 65%) (0%, 52%, 22%, 12%)
(325, 100%, 60%) (0%, 80%, 33%, 0%)	(325, 60%, 50%) (0%, 75%, 31%, 20%)	(325, 60%, 60%) (0%, 57%, 24%, 16%)
(325, 100%, 55%) (0%, 90%, 38%, 0%)	(325, 55%, 50%) (0%, 71%, 30%, 22%)	(325, 55%, 55%) (0%, 62%, 26%, 20%)
(325, 100%, 50%) (0%, 100%, 42%, 0%)	(325, 50%, 50%) (0%, 67%, 28%, 25%)	(325, 50%, 50%) (0%, 67%, 28%, 25%)
(325, 100%, 45%) (0%, 100%, 42%, 10%)	(325, 45%, 50%) (0%, 62%, 26%, 28%)	(325, 45%, 45%) (0%, 62%, 26%, 35%)
(325, 100%, 40%) (0%, 100%, 42%, 20%)	(325, 40%, 50%) (0%, 57%, 24%, 30%)	(325, 40, 40%) (0%, 57%, 24%, 44%)
(325, 100%, 35%) (0%, 100%, 42%, 30%)	(325, 35%, 50%) (0%, 52%, 22%, 32%)	(325, 35%, 35%) (0%, 52%, 22%, 53%)
(325, 100%, 30%) (0%, 100%, 42%, 40%)	(325, 30%, 50%) (0%, 46%, 19%, 35%)	(325, 30%, 30%) (0%, 46%, 19%, 61%)
(325, 100%, 25%) (0%, 100%, 42%, 50%)	(325, 25%, 50%) (0%, 40%, 17%, 38%)	(325, 25%, 25%) (0%, 40%, 17%, 69%)
(325, 100%, 20%) (0%, 100%, 42%, 60%)	(325, 20%, 50%) (0%, 33%, 14%, 40%)	(325, 20%, 20%) (0%, 33%, 14%, 76%)
(325, 100%, 15%) (0%, 100%, 42%, 70%)	(325, 15%, 50%) (0%, 26%, 11%, 43%)	(325, 15%, 15%) (0%, 26%, 11%, 83%)
(325, 100%, 10%) (0%, 100%, 42%, 80%)	(325, 10%, 50%) (0%, 18%, 8%, 45%)	(325, 10%, 10%) (0%, 18%, 8%, 89%)
(325, 100%, 5%) (0%, 100%, 42%, 90%)	(325, 5%, 50%) (0%, 10%, 4%, 47%)	(325, 5%, 5%) (0%, 10%, 4%, 95%)
(325, 100%, 0%) (0%, 0%, 0%, 100%)	(325, 0%, 50%) (0%, 0%, 0%, 50%)	(325, 0%, 0%) (0%, 0%, 0%, 100%)

H = 330, S = X%, L = X%	H = 330, S = X%, L = 50%	H = 330, S = 100%, L = X%
(330, 100%, 100%) (0%, 0%, 0%, 0%)	(330, 100%, 50%) (0%, 100%, 50%, 0%)	(330, 100%, 100%) (0%, 0%, 0%, 0%)
(330, 95%, 95%) (0%, 10%, 5%, 0%)	(330, 95%, 50%) (0%, 97%, 49%, 3%)	(330, 100%, 95%) (0%, 10%, 5%, 0%)
(330, 90%, 90%) (0%, 18%, 9%, 1%)	(330, 90%, 50%) (0%, 95%, 47%, 5%)	(330, 100%, 90%) (0%, 20%, 10%, 0%)
(330, 85%, 85%) (0%, 26%, 13%, 2%)	(330, 85%, 50%) (0%, 92%, 46%, 7%)	(330, 100%, 85%) (0%, 30%, 15%, 0%)
(330, 80%, 80%) (0%, 33%, 17%, 4%)	(330, 80%, 50%) (0%, 89%, 44%, 10%)	(330, 100%, 80%) (0%, 40%, 20%, 0%)
(330, 75%, 75%) (0%, 40%, 20%, 6%)	(330, 75%, 50%) (0%, 86%, 43%, 13%)	(330, 100%, 75%) (0%, 50%, 25%, 0%)
(330, 70%, 70%) (0%, 46%, 23%, 9%)	(330, 70%, 50%) (0%, 82%, 41%, 15%)	(330, 100%, 70%) (0%, 60%, 30%, 0%)
(330, 65%, 65%) (0%, 52%, 26%, 12%)	(330, 65%, 50%) (0%, 79%, 39%, 18%)	(330, 100%, 65%) (0%, 70%, 35%, 0%)
(330, 60%, 60%) (0%, 57%, 29%, 16%)	(330, 60%, 50%) (0%, 75%, 38%, 20%)	(330, 100%, 60%) (0%, 80%, 40%, 0%)
(330, 55%, 55%) (0%, 62%, 31%, 20%)	(330, 55%, 50%) (0%, 71%, 35%, 22%)	(330, 100%, 55%) (0%, 90%, 45%, 0%)
(330, 50%, 50%) (0%, 67%, 33%, 25%)	(330, 50%, 50%) (0%, 67%, 33%, 25%)	(330, 100%, 50%) (0%, 100%, 50%, 0%)
(330, 45%, 45%) (0%, 62%, 31%, 35%)	(330, 45%, 50%) (0%, 62%, 31%, 28%)	(330, 100%, 45%) (0%, 100%, 50%, 10%)
(330, 40, 40%) (0%, 57%, 29%, 44%)	(330, 40%, 50%) (0%, 57%, 29%, 30%)	(330, 100%, 40%) (0%, 100%, 50%, 20%)
(330, 35%, 35%) (0%, 52%, 26%, 53%)	(330, 35%, 50%) (0%, 52%, 26%, 32%)	(330, 100%, 35%) (0%, 100%, 50%, 30%)
(330, 30%, 30%) (0%, 46%, 23%, 61%)	(330, 30%, 50%) (0%, 46%, 23%, 35%)	(330, 100%, 30%) (0%, 100%, 50%, 40%)
(330, 25%, 25%) (0%, 40%, 20%, 69%)	(330, 25%, 50%) (0%, 40%, 20%, 38%)	(330, 100%, 25%) (0%, 100%, 50%, 50%)
(330, 20%, 20%) (0%, 33%, 17%, 76%)	(330, 20%, 50%) (0%, 33%, 17%, 40%)	(330, 100%, 20%) (0%, 100%, 50%, 60%)
(330, 15%, 15%) (0%, 26%, 13%, 83%)	(330, 15%, 50%) (0%, 26%, 13%, 43%)	(330, 100%, 15%) (0%, 100%, 50%, 70%)
(330, 10%, 10%) (0%, 18%, 9%, 89%)	(330, 10%, 50%) (0%, 18%, 9%, 45%)	(330, 100%, 10%) (0%, 100%, 50%, 80%)
(330, 5%, 5%) (0%, 10%, 5%, 95%)	(330, 5%, 50%) (0%, 10%, 5%, 47%)	(330, 100%, 5%) (0%, 100%, 50%, 90%)
(330, 0%, 0%) (0%, 0%, 0%, 100%)	(330, 0%, 50%) (0%, 0%, 0%, 50%)	(330, 100%, 0%) (0%, 0%, 0%, 100%)

H = 335, S = 100%, L = X%	H = 335, S = X%, L = 50%	H = 335, S = X%, L = X%
(335, 100%, 100%) (0%, 0%, 0%, 0%)	(335, 100%, 50%) (0%, 100%, 58%, 0%)	(335, 100%, 100%) (0%, 0%, 0%, 0%)
(335, 100%, 95%) (0%, 10%, 6%, 0%)	(335, 95%, 50%) (0%, 97%, 57%, 3%)	(335, 95%, 95%) (0%, 10%, 6%, 0%)
(335, 100%, 90%) (0%, 20%, 12%, 0%)	(335, 90%, 50%) (0%, 95%, 55%, 5%)	(335, 90%, 90%) (0%, 18%, 11%, 1%)
(335, 100%, 85%) (0%, 30%, 17%, 0%)	(335, 85%, 50%) (0%, 92%, 54%, 7%)	(335, 85%, 85%) (0%, 26%, 15%, 2%)
(335, 100%, 80%) (0%, 40%, 23%, 0%)	(335, 80%, 50%) (0%, 89%, 52%, 10%)	(335, 80%, 80%) (0%, 33%, 19%, 4%)
(335, 100%, 75%) (0%, 50%, 29%, 0%)	(335, 75%, 50%) (0%, 86%, 50%, 13%)	(335, 75%, 75%) (0%, 40%, 23%, 6%)
(335, 100%, 70%) (0%, 60%, 35%, 0%)	(335, 70%, 50%) (0%, 82%, 48%, 15%)	(335, 70%, 70%) (0%, 46%, 27%, 9%)
(335, 100%, 65%) (0%, 70%, 41%, 0%)	(335, 65%, 50%) (0%, 79%, 46%, 18%)	(335, 65%, 65%) (0%, 52%, 30%, 12%)
(335, 100%, 60%) (0%, 80%, 47%, 0%)	(335, 60%, 50%) (0%, 75%, 44%, 20%)	(335, 60%, 60%) (0%, 57%, 33%, 16%)
(335, 100%, 55%) (0%, 90%, 52%, 0%)	(335, 55%, 50%) (0%, 71%, 41%, 22%)	(335, 55%, 55%) (0%, 62%, 36%, 20%)
(335, 100%, 50%) (0%, 100%, 58%, 0%)	(335, 50%, 50%) (0%, 67%, 39%, 25%)	(335, 50%, 50%) (0%, 67%, 39%, 25%)
(335, 100%, 45%) (0%, 100%, 58%, 10%)	(335, 45%, 50%) (0%, 62%, 36%, 28%)	(335, 45%, 45%) (0%, 62%, 36%, 35%)
(335, 100%, 40%) (0%, 100%, 58%, 20%)	(335, 40%, 50%) (0%, 57%, 33%, 30%)	(335, 40, 40%) (0%, 57%, 33%, 44%)
(335, 100%, 35%) (0%, 100%, 58%, 30%)	(335, 35%, 50%) (0%, 52%, 30%, 32%)	(335, 35%, 35%) (0%, 52%, 30%, 53%)
(335, 100%, 30%) (0%, 100%, 58%, 40%)	(335, 30%, 50%) (0%, 46%, 27%, 35%)	(335, 30%, 30%) (0%, 46%, 27%, 61%)
(335, 100%, 25%) (0%, 100%, 58%, 50%)	(335, 25%, 50%) (0%, 40%, 23%, 38%)	(335, 25%, 25%) (0%, 40%, 23%, 69%)
(335, 100%, 20%) (0%, 100%, 58%, 60%)	(335, 20%, 50%) (0%, 33%, 19%, 40%)	(335, 20%, 20%) (0%, 33%, 19%, 76%)
(335, 100%, 15%) (0%, 100%, 58%, 70%)	(335, 15%, 50%) (0%, 26%, 15%, 43%)	(335, 15%, 15%) (0%, 26%, 15%, 83%)
(335, 100%, 10%) (0%, 100%, 58%, 80%)	(335, 10%, 50%) (0%, 18%, 11%, 45%)	(335, 10%, 10%) (0%, 18%, 11%, 89%)
(335, 100%, 5%) (0%, 100%, 58%, 90%)	(335, 5%, 50%) (0%, 10%, 6%, 47%)	(335, 5%, 5%) (0%, 10%, 6%, 95%)
(335, 100%, 0%) (0%, 0%, 0%, 100%)	(335, 0%, 50%) (0%, 0%, 0%, 50%)	(335, 0%, 0%) (0%, 0%, 0%, 100%)

H = 340, S = X%, L = X%	H = 340, S = X%, L = 50%	H = 340, S = 100%, L = X%
(340, 100%, 100%) (0%, 0%, 0%, 0%)	(340, 100%, 50%) (0%, 100%, 67%, 0%)	(340, 100%, 100%) (0%, 0%, 0%, 0%)
(340, 95%, 95%) (0%, 10%, 6%, 0%)	(340, 95%, 50%) (0%, 97%, 65%, 3%)	(340, 100%, 95%) (0%, 10%, 7%, 0%)
(340, 90%, 90%) (0%, 18%, 12%, 1%)	(340, 90%, 50%) (0%, 95%, 63%, 5%)	(340, 100%, 90%) (0%, 20%, 13%, 0%)
(340, 85%, 85%) (0%, 26%, 17%, 2%)	(340, 85%, 50%) (0%, 92%, 61%, 7%)	(340, 100%, 85%) (0%, 30%, 20%, 0%)
(340, 80%, 80%) (0%, 33%, 22%, 4%)	(340, 80%, 50%) (0%, 89%, 59%, 10%)	(340, 100%, 80%) (0%, 40%, 27%, 0%)
(340, 75%, 75%) (0%, 40%, 27%, 6%)	(340, 75%, 50%) (0%, 86%, 57%, 13%)	(340, 100%, 75%) (0%, 50%, 33%, 0%)
(340, 70%, 70%) (0%, 46%, 31%, 9%)	(340, 70%, 50%) (0%, 82%, 55%, 15%)	(340, 100%, 70%) (0%, 60%, 40%, 0%)
(340, 65%, 65%) (0%, 52%, 35%, 12%)	(340, 65%, 50%) (0%, 79%, 53%, 18%)	(340, 100%, 65%) (0%, 70%, 47%, 0%)
(340, 60%, 60%) (0%, 57%, 38%, 16%)	(340, 60%, 50%) (0%, 75%, 50%, 20%)	(340, 100%, 60%) (0%, 80%, 53%, 0%)
(340, 55%, 55%) (0%, 62%, 41%, 20%)	(340, 55%, 50%) (0%, 71%, 47%, 22%)	(340, 100%, 55%) (0%, 90%, 60%, 0%)
(340, 50%, 50%) (0%, 67%, 44%, 25%)	(340, 50%, 50%) (0%, 67%, 44%, 25%)	(340, 100%, 50%) (0%, 100%, 67%, 0%)
(340, 45%, 45%) (0%, 62%, 41%, 35%)	(340, 45%, 50%) (0%, 62%, 41%, 28%)	(340, 100%, 45%) (0%, 100%, 67%, 10%)
(340, 40, 40%) (0%, 57%, 38%, 44%)	(340, 40%, 50%) (0%, 57%, 38%, 30%)	(340, 100%, 40%) (0%, 100%, 67%, 20%)
(340, 35%, 35%) (0%, 52%, 35%, 53%)	(340, 35%, 50%) (0%, 52%, 35%, 32%)	(340, 100%, 35%) (0%, 100%, 67%, 30%)
(340, 30%, 30%) (0%, 46%, 31%, 61%)	(340, 30%, 50%) (0%, 46%, 31%, 35%)	(340, 100%, 30%) (0%, 100%, 67%, 40%)
(340, 25%, 25%) (0%, 40%, 27%, 69%)	(340, 25%, 50%) (0%, 40%, 27%, 38%)	(340, 100%, 25%) (0%, 100%, 67%, 50%)
(340, 20%, 20%) (0%, 33%, 22%, 76%)	(340, 20%, 50%) (0%, 33%, 22%, 40%)	(340, 100%, 20%) (0%, 100%, 67%, 60%)
(340, 15%, 15%) (0%, 26%, 17%, 83%)	(340, 15%, 50%) (0%, 26%, 17%, 43%)	(340, 100%, 15%) (0%, 100%, 67%, 70%)
(340, 10%, 10%) (0%, 18%, 12%, 89%)	(340, 10%, 50%) (0%, 18%, 12%, 45%)	(340, 100%, 10%) (0%, 100%, 67%, 80%)
(340, 5%, 5%) (0%, 10%, 6%, 95%)	(340, 5%, 50%) (0%, 10%, 6%, 47%)	(340, 100%, 5%) (0%, 100%, 67%, 90%)
(340, 0%, 0%) (0%, 0%, 0%, 100%)	(340, 0%, 50%) (0%, 0%, 0%, 50%)	(340, 100%, 0%) (0%, 0%, 0%, 100%)

H = 345, S = 100%, L = X%	H = 345, S = X%, L = 50%	H = 345, S = X%, L = X%
(345, 100%, 100%) (0%, 0%, 0%, 0%)	(345, 100%, 50%) (0%, 100%, 75%, 0%)	(345, 100%, 100%) (0%, 0%, 0%, 0%)
(345, 100%, 95%) (0%, 10%, 8%, 0%)	(345, 95%, 50%) (0%, 97%, 73%, 3%)	(345, 95%, 95%) (0%, 10%, 7%, 0%)
(345, 100%, 90%) (0%, 20%, 15%, 0%)	(345, 90%, 50%) (0%, 95%, 71%, 5%)	(345, 90%, 90%) (0%, 18%, 14%, 1%)
(345, 100%, 85%) (0%, 30%, 23%, 0%)	(345, 85%, 50%) (0%, 92%, 69%, 7%)	(345, 85%, 85%) (0%, 26%, 20%, 2%)
(345, 100%, 80%) (0%, 40%, 30%, 0%)	(345, 80%, 50%) (0%, 89%, 67%, 10%)	(345, 80%, 80%) (0%, 33%, 25%, 4%)
(345, 100%, 75%) (0%, 50%, 38%, 0%)	(345, 75%, 50%) (0%, 86%, 64%, 13%)	(345, 75%, 75%) (0%, 40%, 30%, 6%)
(345, 100%, 70%) (0%, 60%, 45%, 0%)	(345, 70%, 50%) (0%, 82%, 62%, 15%)	(345, 70%, 70%) (0%, 46%, 35%, 9%)
(345, 100%, 65%) (0%, 70%, 52%, 0%)	(345, 65%, 50%) (0%, 79%, 59%, 18%)	(345, 65%, 65%) (0%, 52%, 39%, 12%)
(345, 100%, 60%) (0%, 80%, 60%, 0%)	(345, 60%, 50%) (0%, 75%, 56%, 20%)	(345, 60%, 60%) (0%, 57%, 43%, 16%)
(345, 100%, 55%) (0%, 90%, 67%, 0%)	(345, 55%, 50%) (0%, 71%, 53%, 22%)	(345, 55%, 55%) (0%, 62%, 47%, 20%)
(345, 100%, 50%) (0%, 100%, 75%, 0%)	(345, 50%, 50%) (0%, 67%, 50%, 25%)	(345, 50%, 50%) (0%, 67%, 50%, 25%)
(345, 100%, 45%) (0%, 100%, 75%, 10%)	(345, 45%, 50%) (0%, 62%, 47%, 28%)	(345, 45%, 45%) (0%, 62%, 47%, 35%)
(345, 100%, 40%) (0%, 100%, 75%, 20%)	(345, 40%, 50%) (0%, 57%, 43%, 30%)	(345, 40, 40%) (0%, 57%, 43%, 44%)
(345, 100%, 35%) (0%, 100%, 75%, 30%)	(345, 35%, 50%) (0%, 52%, 39%, 32%)	(345, 35%, 35%) (0%, 52%, 39%, 53%)
(345, 100%, 30%) (0%, 100%, 75%, 40%)	(345, 30%, 50%) (0%, 46%, 35%, 35%)	(345, 30%, 30%) (0%, 46%, 35%, 61%)
(345, 100%, 25%) (0%, 100%, 75%, 50%)	(345, 25%, 50%) (0%, 40%, 30%, 38%)	(345, 25%, 25%) (0%, 40%, 30%, 69%)
(345, 100%, 20%) (0%, 100%, 75%, 60%)	(345, 20%, 50%) (0%, 33%, 25%, 40%)	(345, 20%, 20%) (0%, 33%, 25%, 76%)
(345, 100%, 15%) (0%, 100%, 75%, 70%)	(345, 15%, 50%) (0%, 26%, 20%, 43%)	(345, 15%, 15%) (0%, 26%, 20%, 83%)
(345, 100%, 10%) (0%, 100%, 75%, 80%)	(345, 10%, 50%) (0%, 18%, 14%, 45%)	(345, 10%, 10%) (0%, 18%, 14%, 89%)
(345, 100%, 5%) (0%, 100%, 75%, 90%)	(345, 5%, 50%) (0%, 10%, 7%, 47%)	(345, 5%, 5%) (0%, 10%, 7%, 95%)
(345, 100%, 0%) (0%, 0%, 0%, 100%)	(345, 0%, 50%) (0%, 0%, 0%, 50%)	(345, 0%, 0%) (0%, 0%, 0%, 100%)

H = 350, S = X%, L = X%	H = 350, S = X%, L = 50%	H = 350, S = 100%, L = X%
(350, 100%, 100%) (0%, 0%, 0%, 0%)	(350, 100%, 50%) (0%, 100%, 83%, 0%)	(350, 100%, 100%) (0%, 0%, 0%, 0%)
(350, 95%, 95%) (0%, 10%, 8%, 0%)	(350, 95%, 50%) (0%, 97%, 81%, 3%)	(350, 100%, 95%) (0%, 10%, 8%, 0%)
(350, 90%, 90%) (0%, 18%, 15%, 1%)	(350, 90%, 50%) (0%, 95%, 79%, 5%)	(350, 100%, 90%) (0%, 20%, 17%, 0%)
(350, 85%, 85%) (0%, 26%, 22%, 2%)	(350, 85%, 50%) (0%, 92%, 77%, 7%)	(350, 100%, 85%) (0%, 30%, 25%, 0%)
(350, 80%, 80%) (0%, 33%, 28%, 4%)	(350, 80%, 50%) (0%, 89%, 74%, 10%)	(350, 100%, 80%) (0%, 40%, 33%, 0%)
(350, 75%, 75%) (0%, 40%, 33%, 6%)	(350, 75%, 50%) (0%, 86%, 71%, 13%)	(350, 100%, 75%) (0%, 50%, 42%, 0%)
(350, 70%, 70%) (0%, 46%, 38%, 9%)	(350, 70%, 50%) (0%, 82%, 69%, 15%)	(350, 100%, 70%) (0%, 60%, 50%, 0%)
(350, 65%, 65%) (0%, 52%, 43%, 12%)	(350, 65%, 50%) (0%, 79%, 66%, 18%)	(350, 100%, 65%) (0%, 70%, 58%, 0%)
(350, 60%, 60%) (0%, 57%, 48%, 16%)	(350, 60%, 50%) (0%, 75%, 62%, 20%)	(350, 100%, 60%) (0%, 80%, 67%, 0%)
(350, 55%, 55%) (0%, 62%, 52%, 20%)	(350, 55%, 50%) (0%, 71%, 59%, 22%)	(350, 100%, 55%) (0%, 90%, 75%, 0%)
(350, 50%, 50%) (0%, 67%, 56%, 25%)	(350, 50%, 50%) (0%, 67%, 56%, 25%)	(350, 100%, 50%) (0%, 100%, 83%, 0%)
(350, 45%, 45%) (0%, 62%, 52%, 35%)	(350, 45%, 50%) (0%, 62%, 52%, 28%)	(350, 100%, 45%) (0%, 100%, 83%, 10%)
(350, 40, 40%) (0%, 57%, 48%, 44%)	(350, 40%, 50%) (0%, 57%, 48%, 30%)	(350, 100%, 40%) (0%, 100%, 83%, 20%)
(350, 35%, 35%) (0%, 52%, 43%, 53%)	(350, 35%, 50%) (0%, 52%, 43%, 32%)	(350, 100%, 35%) (0%, 100%, 83%, 30%)
(350, 30%, 30%) (0%, 46%, 38%, 61%)	(350, 30%, 50%) (0%, 46%, 38%, 35%)	(350, 100%, 30%) (0%, 100%, 83%, 40%)
(350, 25%, 25%) (0%, 40%, 35%, 69%)	(350, 25%, 50%) (0%, 40%, 33%, 38%)	(350, 100%, 25%) (0%, 100%, 83%, 50%)
(350, 20%, 20%) (0%, 33%, 28%, 76%)	(350, 20%, 50%) (0%, 33%, 28%, 40%)	(350, 100%, 20%) (0%, 100%, 83%, 60%)
(350, 15%, 15%) (0%, 26%, 22%, 83%)	(350, 15%, 50%) (0%, 26%, 22%, 43%)	(350, 100%, 15%) (0%, 100%, 83%, 70%)
(350, 10%, 10%) (0%, 18%, 15%, 89%)	(350, 10%, 50%) (0%, 18%, 15%, 45%)	(350, 100%, 10%) (0%, 100%, 83%, 80%)
(350, 5%, 5%) (0%, 10%, 8%, 95%)	(350, 5%, 50%) (0%, 10%, 8%, 47%)	(350, 100%, 5%) (0%, 100%, 83%, 90%)
(350, 0%, 0%) (0%, 0%, 0%, 100%)	(350, 0%, 50%) (0%, 0%, 0%, 50%)	(350, 100%, 0%) (0%, 0%, 0%, 100%)

H = 355, S = 100%, L = X%	H = 355, S = X%, L = 50%	H = 355, S = X%, L = X%
(355, 100%, 100%) (0%, 0%, 0%, 0%)	(355, 100%, 50%) (0%, 100%, 92%, 0%)	(355, 100%, 100%) (0%, 0%, 0%, 0%)
(355, 100%, 95%) (0%, 10%, 9%, 0%)	(355, 95%, 50%) (0%, 97%, 89%, 3%)	(355, 95%, 95%) (0%, 10%, 9%, 0%)
(355, 100%, 90%) (0%, 20%, 18%, 0%)	(355, 90%, 50%) (0%, 95%, 87%, 5%)	(355, 90%, 90%) (0%, 18%, 17%, 1%)
(355, 100%, 85%) (0%, 30%, 28%, 0%)	(355, 85%, 50%) (0%, 92%, 84%, 7%)	(355, 85%, 85%) (0%, 26%, 24%, 2%)
(355, 100%, 80%) (0%, 40%, 37%, 0%)	(355, 80%, 50%) (0%, 89%, 81%, 10%)	(355, 80%, 80%) (0%, 33%, 31%, 4%)
(355, 100%, 75%) (0%, 50%, 46%, 0%)	(355, 75%, 50%) (0%, 86%, 79%, 13%)	(355, 75%, 75%) (0%, 40%, 37%, 6%)
(355, 100%, 70%) (0%, 60%, 55%, 0%)	(355, 70%, 50%) (0%, 82%, 75%, 15%)	(355, 70%, 70%) (0%, 46%, 42%, 9%)
(355, 100%, 65%) (0%, 70%, 64%, 0%)	(355, 65%, 50%) (0%, 79%, 72%, 18%)	(355, 65%, 65%) (0%, 52%, 48%, 12%)
(355, 100%, 60%) (0%, 80%, 73%, 0%)	(355, 60%, 50%) (0%, 75%, 69%, 20%)	(355, 60%, 60%) (0%, 57%, 52%, 16%)
(355, 100%, 55%) (0%, 90%, 83%, 0%)	(355, 55%, 50%) (0%, 71%, 65%, 22%)	(355, 55%, 55%) (0%, 62%, 57%, 20%)
(355, 100%, 50%) (0%, 100%, 92%, 0%)	(355, 50%, 50%) (0%, 67%, 61%, 25%)	(355, 50%, 50%) (0%, 67%, 61%, 25%)
(355, 100%, 45%) (0%, 100%, 92%, 10%)	(355, 45%, 50%) (0%, 62%, 57%, 28%)	(355, 45%, 45%) (0%, 62%, 57%, 35%)
(355, 100%, 40%) (0%, 100%, 92%, 20%)	(355, 40%, 50%) (0%, 57%, 52%, 30%)	(355, 40, 40%) (0%, 57%, 52%, 44%)
(355, 100%, 35%) (0%, 100%, 92%, 30%)	(355, 35%, 50%) (0%, 52%, 48%, 32%)	(355, 35%, 35%) (0%, 52%, 48%, 53%)
(355, 100%, 30%) (0%, 100%, 92%, 40%)	(355, 30%, 50%) (0%, 46%, 42%, 35%)	(355, 30%, 30%) (0%, 46%, 42%, 61%)
(355, 100%, 25%) (0%, 100%, 92%, 50%)	(355, 25%, 50%) (0%, 40%, 37%, 38%)	(355, 25%, 25%) (0%, 40%, 37%, 69%)
(355, 100%, 20%) (0%, 100%, 92%, 60%)	(355, 20%, 50%) (0%, 33%, 31%, 40%)	(355, 20%, 20%) (0%, 33%, 31%, 76%)
(355, 100%, 15%) (0%, 100%, 92%, 70%)	(355, 15%, 50%) (0%, 26%, 24%, 43%)	(355, 15%, 15%) (0%, 26%, 24%, 83%)
(355, 100%, 10%) (0%, 100%, 92%, 80%)	(355, 10%, 50%) (0%, 18%, 17%, 45%)	(355, 10%, 10%) (0%, 18%, 17%, 89%)
(355, 100%, 5%) (0%, 100%, 92%, 90%)	(355, 5%, 50%) (0%, 10%, 9%, 47%)	(355, 5%, 5%) (0%, 10%, 9%, 95%)
(355, 100%, 0%) (0%, 0%, 0%, 100%)	(355, 0%, 50%) (0%, 0%, 0%, 50%)	(355, 0%, 0%) (0%, 0%, 0%, 100%)

H = 360, S = X%, L = X%	H = 360, S = X%, L = 50%	H = 360, S = 100%, L = X%
(360, 100%, 100%) (0%, 0%, 0%, 0%)	(360, 100%, 50%) (0%, 100%, 100%, 0%)	(360, 100%, 100%) (0%, 0%, 0%, 0%)
(360, 95%, 95%) (0%, 10%, 10%, 0%)	(360, 95%, 50%) (0%, 97%, 97%, 3%)	(360, 100%, 95%) (0%, 10%, 10%, 0%)
(360, 90%, 90%) (0%, 18%, 18%, 1%)	(360, 90%, 50%) (0%, 95%, 95%, 5%)	(360, 100%, 90%) (0%, 20%, 20%, 0%)
(360, 85%, 85%) (0%, 26%, 26%, 2%)	(360, 85%, 50%) (0%, 92%, 92%, 7%)	(360, 100%, 85%) (0%, 30%, 30%, 0%)
(360, 80%, 80%) (0%, 33%, 33%, 4%)	(360, 80%, 50%) (0%, 89%, 89%, 10%)	(360, 100%, 80%) (0%, 40%, 40%, 0%)
(360, 75%, 75%) (0%, 40%, 40%, 6%)	(360, 75%, 50%) (0%, 86%, 86%, 13%)	(360, 100%, 75%) (0%, 50%, 50%, 0%)
(360, 70%, 70%) (0%, 46%, 46%, 9%)	(360, 70%, 50%) (0%, 82%, 82%, 15%)	(360, 100%, 70%) (0%, 60%, 60%, 0%)
(360, 65%, 65%) (0%, 52%, 52%, 12%)	(360, 65%, 50%) (0%, 79%, 79%, 18%)	(360, 100%, 65%) (0%, 70%, 70%, 0%)
(360, 60%, 60%) (0%, 57%, 57%, 16%)	(360, 60%, 50%) (0%, 75%, 75%, 20%)	(360, 100%, 60%) (0%, 80%, 80%, 0%)
(360, 55%, 55%) (0%, 62%, 62%, 20%)	(360, 55%, 50%) (0%, 71%, 71%, 22%)	(360, 100%, 55%) (0%, 90%, 90%, 0%)
(360, 50%, 50%) (0%, 67%, 67%, 25%)	(360, 50%, 50%) (0%, 67%, 67%, 25%)	(360, 100%, 50%) (0%, 100%, 100%, 0%)
(360, 45%, 45%) (0%, 62%, 62%, 35%)	(360, 45%, 50%) (0%, 62%, 62%, 28%)	(360, 100%, 45%) (0%, 100%, 100%, 10%)
(360, 40, 40%) (0%, 57%, 57%, 44%)	(360, 40%, 50%) (0%, 57%, 57%, 30%)	(360, 100%, 40%) (0%, 100%, 100%, 20%)
(360, 35%, 35%) (0%, 52%, 52%, 53%)	(360, 35%, 50%) (0%, 52%, 52%, 32%)	(360, 100%, 35%) (0%, 100%, 100%, 30%)
(360, 30%, 30%) (0%, 46%, 46%, 61%)	(360, 30%, 50%) (0%, 46%, 46%, 35%)	(360, 100%, 30%) (0%, 100%, 100%, 40%)
(360, 25%, 25%) (0%, 40%, 40%, 69%)	(360, 25%, 50%) (0%, 40%, 40%, 38%)	(360, 100%, 25%) (0%, 100%, 100%, 50%)
(360, 20%, 20%) (0%, 33%, 33%, 76%)	(360, 20%, 50%) (0%, 33%, 33%, 40%)	(360, 100%, 20%) (0%, 100%, 100%, 60%)
(360, 15%, 15%) (0%, 26%, 26%, 83%)	(360, 15%, 50%) (0%, 26%, 26%, 43%)	(360, 100%, 15%) (0%, 100%, 100%, 70%)
(360, 10%, 10%) (0%, 18%, 18%, 89%)	(360, 10%, 50%) (0%, 18%, 18%, 45%)	(360, 100%, 10%) (0%, 100%, 100%, 80%)
(360, 5%, 5%) (0%, 10%, 10%, 95%)	(360, 5%, 50%) (0%, 10%, 10%, 47%)	(360, 100%, 5%) (0%, 100%, 100%, 90%)
(360, 0%, 0%) (0%, 0%, 0%, 100%)	(360, 0%, 50%) (0%, 0%, 0%, 50%)	(360, 100%, 0%) (0%, 0%, 0%, 100%)

Made in the USA
Monee, IL
05 November 2026

67384058R00048